CAR
Culture

CAR
Culture

Frances Basham and Bob Ughetti
with text by
Paul Rambali

A DELILAH BOOK
Distributed by The Putnam Publishing Group,
New York

A Delilah Book
Delilah Communications Ltd.
118 East 25th Street
New York, N.Y. 10010

Copyright © 1984 by Plexus Publishing Limited

ISBN: 0–933328–74–5
Library of Congress Catalog Card Number:
83–45221

First published in the United States of America in
1984 by Delilah Communications Ltd.

Originally published in Great Britain in 1984 by
Plexus Publishing Limited.

Cover design and painting by Bob Ughetti

Photograph taken by Harry
Chase for the *Los Angeles
Times* in May, 1962. The
original caption reads: 'Drag
Race check up – Automobile
drivers are questioned by
police in a surprise raid
Tuesday night on drag races
being staged by youths on
Vista Del Mar in Playa Del
Rey. More than 200 youths
were watching the 100 mph
drag races before police
cordoned off the street.
Thirty-eight were taken to
Venice Division Station for
booking on curfew or traffic
regulation violations.'

CONTENTS

INTRODUCTION 1

ROAD DREAMS

On a hot night in 1940, outside an apartment house in Denver, Colorado, the romance began. Two teenage boys were looking for a car to steal. At the curb, fat and shiny with a split windshield and lean chrome ribs, stood a '38 Oldsmobile sedan, its windows open. The Oldsmobile was the first and, like many firsts, it was not won without some fumbling.

The car was equipped, said the brochures, with many new and exciting features. The controls were set away from the dash on bullhorn-shaped dials. Earlier that evening, John had boasted that he knew all about cars. Now, as he slid under the leather seat and glanced up at the unfamiliar layout, his breezy nerve began to ebb.

From behind a tree, Neal watched, unaware that his initiation into this coveted new thrill was not going as smoothly as promised. He watched as first the lights, then the radio, then the wipers – everything, it seemed, except the engine – came to life. Suddenly, inadvertently, a torn lead touched earth, shattering the darkness with the sound of the horn.

Pressed close to the tree, his temples pounding against the bark, Neal saw the other boy run to the end of the block, leaving the car door hanging culpably and glaringly open. The seconds passed, then the minutes . . . Nothing happened; no shouts, no sirens, no searchlights. The panic subsided, slowly returning to the level of fear, which was itself the spice of renewed bravado.

This time, both boys got into the car. Carefully, they crossed the two most promising leads, and heard the engine spin, catch and rumble to attention. The merest touch of the foot was enough to send the powerful car coursing down the quiet Denver streets, teenage hands gripping the wheel as if it were a trophy. The two boys had wrested an adult experience, a taste of power and freedom, from a grindingly slow world.

They finally left the car near an army base to the south of town, having stalled the engine and drained the battery trying to start up again. A few days later, still tingling from his adventure, Neal came around a corner to find . . . a brand new Mercury with the keys dangling!

He burned rubber for most of the first mile, unable to control the surging engine. Wading through a three-phase traffic signal with his motor racing and his tyres squealing, jamming the accelerator, grating the gears, the fourteen-year-old Neal Cassady was much too preoccupied to notice his future unfolding like the road before him, much too busy coaxing the Mercury to yield as he would soon be coaxing a schoolgirl, tempted by the opportunity the Mercury provided to grow up too soon.

By the time he was twenty-one – when, to mark the occasion, he swore off such illicit pleasures – Cassady reckoned to have driven some 500 stolen cars, either borrowed from a parking lot for the purposes of a test drive, or taken for a longer joyride, or sometimes altered and kept for a few weeks. Five hundred cars. It probably wasn't many more than any other major delinquent might boast of on his graduation from the street-corner class, but it would do for a start.

From then on, cars were bought, leased, borrowed and driven; old cars, new cars, all kinds of cars, in endless, restless succession. Cassady drove and drove, from coast to coast and back, through towns that blinked on the map to cities that shone in the distance, through a long list of girlfriends with innocent back-porch names, through two marriages, and on through the pages of beat literature.

Had you been travelling down a certain highway in the winter of 1950 you might have been privileged to see a '49 Hudson Super-Six Club Coupé, on which only the first instalment had been paid, covered in road dust and heading south out of Jersey with the radio tuned to station WJZ broadcasting live jazz from the newly-opened Birdland. With one hand on the wheel at twelve o'clock and the other beating the dashboard in time to the music, Neal Cassady could feel the old adventure stirring anew. Beside him sat Marylou, her knees pressed against his, her eyes bright with the same excitement; and beside her, Jack Kerouac, thinking about his novel.

When it was published in 1957, *On the Road* became an overnight axiom of the American intellectual outlook of the time; and its inspiration, Neal Cassady, the highbrow tourist's epitome of the native modern hero. Kerouac based the character of Dean Moriarty on his pal Cassady. Dean was a true raw natural, whose car was Parker's saxophone, whose life was one long four-wheel drift – a rootless, hungry search for nothing so gaudy as the Promised Land.

A Ford Victoria Tudor, 1931.

The V8 Ford of the early thirties was destined to become a custom classic. Introduced in 1932 in reply to the popular Chevrolet Six, it was available in fourteen body styles, not counting the commercial variants. *Above:* A near-original 1932 Roadster, later to become the favourite of the fifties hot-rodder. *Below:* A Ford Model A Tudor Sedan. In the five years between the end of the Model T and the introduction of the V8, nearly five million Tudor Sedans were built.

In 1934 the Ford V8 acquired a new straightened grille, an improvement on the previous concave grille which perfected the front end of an already classic car. A favourite with today's restorers, replacement parts for this particular model are rumoured to sell for their equivalent value in precious metals.

The 1957 Chevrolet, a car that would go on to break records, hearts and wallets before its day was done. The redesigned front grille merged into this front bumper and by 1957 the tail fin had arrived.

'"Whooee!" yelled Dean. "Here we go!" And he hunched over the wheel and gunned her; he was back in his element, everybody could see that. We were all delighted, we all realised that we were leaving confusion and nonsense behind and performing our one and noble function of the time, move. And we moved!' – Jack Kerouac, *On the Road*

And so, too, did the greater part of teenage America. Motivated by the same restless urge, the same new appetites, the same tearaway blood, but with no beat authors around to chronicle their disaffection, and with copies of *Hop-Up* instead of Sartre's *La Nausée* in the back pockets of their jeans.

The dilemma of a bored and static existence that Neal Cassady as Dean Moriarty was forever trying to outrun in *On the Road* – in what was an echo of the fugitive motorised gangster flights of pre-war folklore – struck deep at the undergraduate emotions of 1957. The road had long been the only solace for a soul determined to run all of society's red lights, as it was for Neal Cassady. Though he had committed no crime (or at least no felony) he had elected for himself the romantic fate of all those *film noir* characters, the sons and daughters of Bonnie and Clyde, pursued by their own shadows across deserted midnight roads.

If Kerouac's Dean was a symbol of intellectual rebellion, another Dean had already become, in the 1955 film *Rebel Without a Cause*, the face of adolescent revolt. It was this film that first brought home to middle America the aberrant uses of the auto in teenage hands, albeit with a plot that finally affirmed the sanctity of all that its lost hero seemed ready to overthrow.

There was, for instance, the infamous, 'chicken race' sequence, a hoodlum nightmare in which two stolen cars were raced headlong towards the edge of a cliff. It ends with Jimmy (James Dean) leaping from his car just in time to see Buzz, who had provoked the whole affair, catch his leather jacket in the door and go plunging into hoodlum oblivion. No doubt a genuine punk would have spat on the moral of the episode. Nevertheless, it was here that the world first confronted the psychology behind the stripped-down, souped-up '32 Ford, the car that was to hot-rodding what the Fender guitar was to rock'n'roll.

Introduced in 1932 to replace the Model A, it housed under a slim, louvred hood the first Ford Flathead V8 engine. Available as a sedan or a roadster with a rumble seat, the new Ford was a perfect, compact expression of the desired proportions of the day.

To turn one of these babies into a rod, you simply removed the front wheel arches, the two running boards and the engine cowl, and then tickled that motor until it sounded exactly right – a baritone V8 roar. That was all you did – for the time being . . .

Far more pressing concerns were keeping the pack of plain Luckies tucked in the sleeve of the white T-shirt, getting the grease out of the fingernails and getting another sort of grease into the hair. Then, after all *these* problems had been overcome, there was the one that had driven Neal Cassady all the way across the continent and back and now hung like a broken high-tension cable spilling a wild charge into the air: the problem of what to *do* tonight!

Chuck Berry is on the radio, America is about to put a monkey into space, and all is well with the world. The teenager has just been discovered, living in a teenage idyll, where wheels are clean and clothes are neat and rock'n'roll will never die. With these articles of teenage faith as yet unclouded by Elvis' entry into the army or the army's entry into the Bay of Pigs, it was enough to drive out into the clear teenage night and do nothing much in particular, just cruise. The night, after all, was young, and so warm and certain that it seemed it would last for ever.

The only agony was . . . what to do with it? Look for some action maybe, a race, a challenge, a way to ignite some of that pent-up teenage octane; pull up at the lights next to a lead sled and invite the owner to choke on your dual exhausts. Well, it *could* happen, but be cool, be like James Dean; he didn't go *looking* for a race. *Nah* . . . Do nothing. Just cruise, with the window down and the breeze rustling the hairs of a lazily protruding elbow; cruise past the girls in their Capri pants and pony tails walking arm in arm, past the diner where hamburgers sizzle on an open griddle and down the road apiece, past the gas stations and the motels with their neons winking at adult experiences, to the drive-in. If the year is 1958 then the chances are that *Thunder Road* is showing.

Thunder Road left a deep scar on those who saw it then, especially those to whom the film was signalling a secret and plaintive message as it lingered just a few seconds longer than necessary on the super-charged Flathead V8 of its hero's grey '50 Ford Custom Tudor.

Produced by and starring Robert Mitchum, *Thunder Road* is the ballad of Luke Doolin, a backwoods son who returns from the war to find organised crime muscling in on the family's illegal liquor still. Luke is the best backroad lightning driver in the country, able to out-corner any revenue man. The film opens with a high-speed chase through the foothills that ends as Luke throws the Ford into a screaming 180-degree bootleg slide.

Luke emerges as a lone, obsessive figure. He has

seen too much of the world ever to return to the grace of the hills. Driving the road at night is his only refuge; his family and his Ford the only things to which he allows himself any final allegiance. Twice he warns mechanics to whom the car is entrusted that if they so much as touch the engine, he'll personally break their legs.

Beyond its political aspects, deeper than the drama of changing and conflicting values, beyond even its merit as a *noir* thriller, *Thunder Road* is a rare and potent expression of the poetry of the road. 'It's a film,' wrote critic Richard Thompson, 'made for those among us who have felt the mystery and elation of driving – not being in a car, but driving – a road at night . . .' A film, as he rightly infers, for *initiates*; offering a lament for the loneliness and disruption that the road has ultimately caused, and a homage to its solitary recompense, the never-ending rhythm of the tarmac and the sublime joy of motion – but not of arrival.

It is also a film that suggests – as Kerouac suggested of Cassady in *On the Road* – that there can be a kind of metaphysical relationship between car and driver; not just in terms of skill and dash as is the case with a racing driver (who, after all, is a professional, familiar with the special requirements of the race and practising on empty circuits for days and weeks) but in the

A 1952 issue of *Hop Up* magazine.

Above: A 1938 Chevrolet Master Deluxe. *Below:* A 1940 Ford V8 – a popular car with customisers and hot-rodders because of its uncluttered appearance.

Above: Twelve cylinders of unabashed luxury from a 1931/2 Auburn. *Below:* Hood (bonnet) detail of a 1940 Packard Super-8.

sense of a merging of being, finally arriving at the point reached by Luke Doolin and Dean Moriarty where the road is existence itself, with no league points to be won, nothing else to do but *drive*.

And Luke Doolin, like Dean Moriarty, was also a character based (though rather more loosely) on a real person. The intellectuals had Neal Cassady, but the good buddies had Junior Johnson, a legendary driver on the southern stock-car tracks of the late 1950s and early 1960s, who took on and, barring breakdowns, usually beat all-comers in their factory-sponsored hard-chargers with his lone '57 Chevy 327ci V8.

Johnson had learned his skills running car loads of moonshine. To facilitate this activity he developed the bootleg slide: faced with a road block, you slam a fast-moving car into second gear, pull the wheel to full lock, and gun the throttle hard, causing the car to about-face in a long straight skid and accelerate off the way it came. He adapted this technique to a more lucrative and legal career on the dirt track, going into bends without braking in a controlled skid that sent a telltale storm of dust up into the stands. Johnson's reputation as a driver of white lightning (and for this he preferred a super-charged Oldsmobile) had reached hallowed proportions by the time he arrived on the stock car circuit. The stories of his uncanny ability to control an automobile, his bravura high-speed antics on the backroads of North Carolina, marked him out as an instinctive genius, a natural-born blacktop demon.

In the days before the motor car, such an idea – that the man could become so attuned to the machine, and the machine so attuned to the man – would have seemed sinister and even blasphemous. It implies an anthropomorphic identity for the car, as though it were imbued with a living, responsive personality – like its predecessor, the horse. And yet even today, when mass production has eliminated most of the quirks of various models, car manufacturers, especially the makers of fast, well-engineered cars, seek to suggest this very thing – a preposterous idea on the face of it – that a machine can be alive to your touch, your moods, your needs; can become, in your possession, an extension of your very self.

It's a notion that is most readily understandable in connection with speed – what Aldous Huxley called the only genuinely modern pleasure – but it has spread, like the mechanical developments of the racetrack, right across the highways; to the point where the functional aspects of cars are subordinate to their supposed or attributed character. This is either ascribable to the power of advertising or the power of imagination, probably to both.

For imagine, if you will, the first sight of the thing in the late 1800s: a wild, surging, noisy, unpredictable monster with the directional stability of a headless chicken. It had to be ridden, mastered, overcome, controlled, like the poor animal that it replaced. Those who could were able to sip the century's strongest draught . . .

> 'Consider the man on horseback, and I have been a man on horseback for most of my life. Well, mostly he is a good man, but there is a change in him as soon as he mounts. Every man on horseback is an arrogant man, however gentle he may be on foot. The man in the automobile is one thousand times as dangerous. I tell you, it will engender absolute selfishness in mankind if the driving of automobiles becomes common. It will breed violence on a scale never seen before. It will mark the end of the family as we know it, the three or four generations living happily in one home. It will destroy the sense of neighbourhood and the true sense of nation. It will create giantized cankers of cities, false opulence of suburbs, ruinized countryside, and unhealthy conglomerations of specialized farming and manufacturing. It will breed rootlessness and immorality. It will make every man a tyrant.' – R. A. Lafferty, *Interurban Queen*

But in the arena of speed, it created a very glamorous fellow indeed. Some drivers, like Tazio Nuvolari and later Stirling Moss, became national heroes, a species of supermen, who had touched what aircraft test-pilots call 'the outside of the envelope', who were able to guide a car at well over 100 mph through the ideal line of a bend, each degree of road camber necessitating a fractional adjustment, with centrifugal forces displacing the weight of the car to the point where it is held to the road by the physical equivalent of a piece of cotton – plus whatever traction the hot rubber tyres could provide. Judging these ratios of velocity, weight, engine revs and bearing strengths in a seamless, continuous, instinctive computation required a feeling for the car and the road, an uninterrupted union of nerve and metal, of near-mystical dimensions.

There are few sports as perilous as Grand Prix racing. Of the thirty-two drivers who had won Grand Prix races by the end of the first twenty years of the championship, eight had subsequently lost their lives in their cars. Then and now, even as the toll continues to rise, the popularity of Grand Prix racing is unabated, and it's probably this very spectre that the crowds come to watch. There is an obvious, immutable link between speed and danger, creating a double exhilaration: the catapult blast of acceleration, straight into the looming embrace of fear.

The car that would do this, that could provide this naked thrill, was what small groups of crackpot amateurs and dedicated engineers in Europe and the US had been attempting to build since the turn of the century, whether by modifying the given or by starting from an empty chassis. In the decades that followed the Second World War, driving became virtually America's unofficial national sport, as throughout the south, all over the mid-west and right across to the Pacific, kids could be seen disappearing into the innards of their hot-rods and jalopies looking for that elusive race tune.

It's worth briefly speculating on the dark side of this quest: the odd truth that the car chase and the car crash are enduring sources of both morbid and comic entertainment. The tradition of endearingly cata-strophic automobiles (familiar to children everywhere) probably stems from the great silent comedies – the cranked-up chases of the Keystone Kops, Stan and Ollie's collapsible Model TS – and perhaps the first decades of the car really were that zany.

The adult fascination with car chases and car crashes, especially car crashes, is less easy to explain. From the hazardous real-life spectacle of Grand Prix to the demolition derbies of films like *The French Connection* and *Bullitt* (in which Peter Yates used the novel trick of fixing cameras inside, underneath and on top of the super-charged Mustang driven by Steve McQueen), the car chase and potential crash exert a compelling pressure on a dim corner of the psyche. There was also *Duel*, the signpost of a hitherto unsuspected paranoia, wherein a menacing articulated truck chooses, for an undisclosed reason, to attack a car driven by an unassuming travelling salesman (Dennis Weaver) along an empty highway. It's a film many people recall with a shudder.

But *Duel* was untypical of this morbid excitement. So where does it spring from? In the case of the high-speed chase or circuit race, it is most likely the vicarious experience of danger, second-hand, but near enough. In the event of the peril actually materialising, it is perhaps partly a horrifying reminder of human fragility, an abrupt and startling negation of all the advertising copy, all the status associations, all the pleasure, pride and pomp of gleaming chrome and cellulose paint suddenly reduced to a mangled bloody wreck.

The blackest realisation of this stark overturning of the idolatry of the automobile was J. G. Ballard's novel *Crash*. The narrator cruises the motorway intersections around London airport in a state of numb, feverish, sexually-charged anticipation of a possible crash, imagining the bent, injured and de-formed bodies of cars and women. Ballard, in one shocking imaginative blow, upsets all the glamour and sexuality of cars, the accumulated associations of virile sportsters, libidinous limousines, backseat teenage petting and mobilised amorality.

His malodorous book prompts the question of why and how the motor car acquired a sexual mystique in the first place. The car came into widespread use in the 1920s, an age that marked a notable swing in social mores. Commentators of the time, especially those in the pulpit (looking out on a flock that was slowly yielding to the adventure of Sunday motoring), were quick to associate the two. Indeed, the motor car must have facilitated more than a few amorous adventures as well. It would go on to become a love trap, a love substitute, and even a love object.

The sexuality of cars is simply a reflection of the sexuality of status. Wealth is sexy. Since it was only the rich who could initially afford to own an automobile, it inevitably became a very sexy attribute. From then on, the whole appeal of cars came to be bound up with status, and with it their sex appeal, if any.

Over and above the purely functional aspect – which rapidly became such a commonplace that it was hardly even considered – and outside the heady realm of speed, the attraction of one motor car as opposed to another was part of an intricate tissue of petty envy. Before mass production and later mass marketing, merely to own a car was sufficient. These early cars tended to be lavish, sumptuous vehicles, the decadent playthings of the idle rich. Motoring was the pleasure of gentlemen, and it was the done thing at the turn of the century to have one's car made to order like one's suits or one's sporting guns. A manufacturer would supply the chassis and engine, then the customer would appoint a recommended coach-builder to con-struct the body. Every detail of the coachwork would be exactly and extravagantly specified according to the requirements of the social season or the sporting calendar or Madam's latest whim – and the coach-builder would set to work with the care and patience of the craftsman he traditionally was. As late as the mid-1910s, when the seeds of a mass market had already been sown by the development in France of the so-called 'light' car for sports events, this approach was still the rule.

In the years that followed, while the humbler means and aspirations of the middle-income buyer would put

'Ever since the first models rolled out of the factory, the car has been seen as an extension of personality. But the standardised variety of the production line was evidently not enough for some people. They would find their own means of self-expression, their own source of self-esteem, in the custom car.'

an end to all but a few of the many bespoke car makers, the demand for superlative personalised transport was, nevertheless, still strong among the flamboyant rich, the stars of stage and screen, the other dazzling creatures who set the pace of the times.

Josephine Baker, the toast of Negrophile Paris in the 1920s, travelled to her engagements in an open Voisin tourer, painted brown and upholstered in brown snakeskin, reflecting to near perfection, it was said, the shade of her own skin. Sonia Delauney, a high fashion clothes designer of the same era, had her cars painted to match the patterns of her clothes: vivid geometric and abstract designs, jumbled alphabets and mosaics. Describing Iris Storm's car in his jazz-age novel *The Green Hat*, Michael Arlen wrote:

> **'Like a huge yellow insect that had dropped to earth from a butterfly civilisation, this car, gallant and suave, rested in the lowly silence of the Shepherd Market night. Open as a yacht, it wore a great shining bonnet; and as though in proud flight over the heads of scores of phantom horses, was that silver stork by which the gentle may be pleased to know that they have just escaped death beneath the wheels of an Hispano-Suiza car.'**

… An Hispano-Suiza H6B, no less, introduced by the Spanish firm in 1919 and variously described as 'an architectural masterpiece bristling with brilliant innovations', and, more poignantly, 'beautiful as a tear drop on a movie star's face'. The propensity of movie idols – always aware of the publicity value of such a flourish – to be seen only in the most grandiose, vainglorious of vehicles would later be parodied by F. Scott Fitzgerald in his story *The Diamond as Big as the Ritz*: 'Its body was of gleaming metal, richer than nickel and lighter than silver … The upholstery consisted of a thousand minute and exquisite tapestries of silk, woven with jewels and embroideries, and set upon a background of cloth of gold.'

Here was status multiplied by folly and doubled by reckless ostentation! The car was such a perfect, outward symbol of rank and position that it was bound to be coveted, in any shape or form, by the great unwheeled – who, while they could only dream of a Duesenberg Tourer or a Jordan Playboy – were willing to mortgage their house in return for just a kiss of the glamour. Asked why they had bought a car when they didn't even have a bathtub, a housewife in *Middletown*, R. and H. Lynd's classic social study of the 1920s, replied: 'You can't drive to town in a bathtub!'

For the time being, the benefits the motor car offered – mobility, autonomy, freedom (and any car could confer them) – were quite enough. The potential opening up of the possibilities of life, the exotic pleasure of travel (until then a prerogative of the rich) and the countryside idylls that were the mainstay of early automobile advertisements were all that was needed, if anything were needed at all, to persuade people to buy a car. But as the market reached a temporary saturation point in the mid 1920s (something the manufacturers couldn't or wouldn't recognise – contributing in part to the great crash of 1929) the advertisers began to look for something else to sell.

It was no longer enough to emphasise freedom and prestige, or even performance or reliability, since everyone else was painting much the same picture on much the same canvas. Sales departments started to press for something more novel. A policy was instituted by some companies of annual model changes, swapping lights, fittings, extras and other small details, and every so often retooling for an entirely new body, as well as offering an increasing variety of engine options. General Motors, in particular, became expert at conjuring a new model from the old, and the annual motor shows were soon the scenes of jealous unveilings to an eager and interested public. Status was no longer a matter merely of owning or not owning an automobile, but of which automobile you owned. The strategy of planned obsolescence was also partly a result of this cunning solution to a marketing crisis, with whose legacy we live to this day.

Every car says something about its owner – it's an advertiser's truism. Each car carries with it a set of assumptions, ascribed partly by advertising, partly by pricing, and partly by where a particular model falls in the market – in other words, and to the eternal dismay of the manufacturers, partly by public taste. There are generic classifications that immediately bring to mind a specific class of person: the executive car, the family car, the sports car, the runabout. And within each of these groupings, there is a further infinite subdivision of status.

A huge industry of metal, rubber and plastic, the manufacturing base of a large part of the world economy, rests underneath this pyramid of caste, catering to the young man's desire for a fast, aggressive, muscular coupé; the young woman's fancy for a smart, dainty compact; the middle-aged man's need for a large, reassuring, luxurious saloon.

In his story *Romance in a 21st Century Parking Lot*, Robert F. Young takes this syndrome to its absurd conclusion. He foretells of an age in which the car, reduced in size to a small, mobile shell of metal, has become the primary clothing of the body. In the showrooms, there are changing booths for people to try on a new car. Predictably, Dad chooses a big sedan, Mom a stationwagon, while Sis wants a bright new convertible. The figurehead of this society is a cross between a smooth-talking unctuous car salesman and Big Brother, who ensures that fashions in car clothes are constantly changing and relies on peer pressure to do the rest. To be seen in an old, crumpled model is like wearing a ragged, outdated suit or dress. To be without a car is the equivalent of going naked.

It's unnecessary to go to such an extreme, though, to see that the car has become a prime expression of taste and aspiration, and thus a strong indication, to those who can read the code (which is almost everybody old enough to own one), of personality – or more correctly, though luckily no one ever consciously thinks about it in this way – of how you would like others to see you.

This idea – that the car is an extension of the person – has spread throughout the motorised world. It has formed the framework of a new hierarchy of status. But in the 1950s the standardised variety of the production line was apparently not enough for some personalities – poor people, young people and fringe people mostly, to whom status was either denied outright or else offered like a carrot only to be contemptuously rejected. These people would find their own means of self-expression, their own source of self-esteem, in the hot-rod and custom car, picking through the wreckage of dented chrome and tangled metal to create a spectacular fusion of wrench and reverie, a wild and often unwitting subversion of everything the latest showroom model ever stood for.

It was to be a loose and motley fellowship – white-trash southern boys, debarred and disaffected blacks, Chicanos, delinquents, the alienated sons of the middle class, poets of the road and aesthetes of speed – determined to burn rubber in the face of the myopic uniform suburban dream.

Casting around for an appropriate euphemism by the time the activity had taken hold in the mid 1950s, somebody coined the phrase 'alternative' cars. It was the first time the word had been used to describe a sub-culture, but it couldn't even begin to describe the magnificent chaos that had been let loose.

An Austin Ruby.

A 1950 Ford.

CHAPTER 2

CAR WARS

In 1924, *Motor* magazine asked Thomas Edison: 'If the automobile develops in the next twenty-five years at the same rate as it has in the past twenty-five years, what will be the most startling transformation in everyday life?' The famous American inventor must have thought long and hard before replying: 'Everybody who can will go out camping in the summer.'

Mass car culture was, by then, already well established in the United States. The beaches of Florida and Southern California were thriving, opened up, like the rest of the country, by the sacred constitutional right of automobility. In 1927, for the first time replacement sales exceeded sales to new owners. The Model T Ford was finally superseded after nearly twenty years by the Model A, and Sir Henry Seagrave became the fastest man on wheels when he reached 200 mph in his 1,000-hp Sunbeam at Daytona Beach. Here was the tangible evidence, and the intangible flavour, of the great romance.

The US at that time boasted eighty per cent of the world's motor vehicles – more than half of them Fords. America was miles ahead, with a ratio of 5.3 people to every one motor vehicle, followed by New Zealand (10.5:1), Canada (10.7:1), Australia (16:1), Argentina (43:1), and then France and Britain both with ratios of 44:1. Germany had 169 people to every one motor vehicle, while in the USSR the figure was 7,010:1. One of these was a requisitioned Tsarist Rolls-Royce that Lenin kept for his personal use. Foreign critics found this very amusing, but obviously the very fact that he had a car at all was massively inegalitarian.

Curiously, the production line methods, and in particular the $5 eight-hour day instituted at Ford plants in order to produce the Model T, were the envy of revolutionary Russia. *Pravda* published articles entitled 'The Fordisation of Russian Factories'. Henry Ford's *My Life and Work* was used as a textbook in Soviet colleges. The great man himself, for his part, was not widely known for endorsing trade unions. A shrewder version of the paternal nineteenth-century capitalist, he would have been horrified at the thought of a Ford factory co-op.

By the time Henry Ford retired his Model T in response to a falling market share, most of the crucial refinements to the motor car had already been introduced. Closed bodies (making the car an all-year proposition), shock absorbers and pneumatic tyres (making it a more comfortable prospect), electric starters (making it easier for the weaker sex), and automatic windscreen wipers and four-wheel hydraulic brakes (making it possible to see a hazard and perhaps even stop in time) were all virtual industry standards. The Cadillac of 1928 featured syncromesh gears and safety glass. Drop-frame construction was yet to come. (This was the dropping between the axles of the passenger cell, which lowered the centre of gravity and thus improved road-holding, but put an end to the chest-high bonnet lines and the feeling of climbing aboard rather than simply getting into a vintage car.) The world would also have to wait a little longer for automatic transmission, air conditioning, central locking, stereos and seat belts. But, basically, the car of 1930 had more in common with the cars of fifty years later than those of as little as ten years before.

From then on, it was merely a matter of improving the existing – revision rather than revolution. The internal combustion engine, with its multitude of moving parts, has been called the perfection of a bad idea. Engines became lighter and stronger, achieving higher compression and more power for their size and weight – largely the fruits of aircraft engine development during the Second World War. Braking systems became more effective with the increasing use of disc/drum combinations, while suspension layout and steering geometry benefited, like all other aspects of the mechanical design of cars, from the experiments of the racetrack.

In the minds of the vast majority of buyers, though, the aesthetics of engineering are secondary, even irrelevant, to the aesthetics of styling. The fact that one often governs the other (and that the mechanics of a car must be more important than its looks) is usually lost or twisted in the copywriter's confection of image and jargon. A minor mechanical change dressed up in pseudo-technical language is sufficient to baffle and impress the customer. The gleam and curve of the metal are the most important things.

But even here, and perhaps above all here, logic and necessity play only a small part. The architectural dictum that form should follow function rarely entered

'The job of the car designer was and is to stimulate and satisfy desire; to express an ideal of proportion and line and to provide a symbol of the aspirations of the age.' A 1936 Oldsmobile.

The basic hot-rod variations, all three based on 1932 Fords which were cheap and plentiful in the fifties. Removing the fenders (wings) was all that was necessary to achieve the coveted contours of a little deuce coupe, although these cars were often a mish-mash of Model A and B body panels, grilles and trim. *Above:* A Model B 1932 Ford. *Below:* A Model B 1932 Ford. *Opposite:* A Model A 1932 Ford.

The front grille of a 1938 Ford V8. Its purpose was no longer simply to allow air through to cool the radiator, but to suggest flight and motion, streamlined styling which was obtained by extending the horizontal slots of the grille to blend into the sides.

the thoughts of most car designers until very recently. Nor, until recently, did it need to. Their job was, and is, to stimulate and satisfy desire; to express an ideal of proportion and line, and to provide a symbol of the aspirations of the age. Roland Barthes called their work the exact equivalent of the great Gothic cathedrals: 'The supreme creation of an era, conceived with passion by unknown artists, and consumed in image if not in usage by a whole population which appropriates them as purely magical objects.'

To begin with, the car designer's problem is one of proportion and line. A car must not appear too cumbersome or top-heavy, it mustn't appear to overhang the axles too far or bulge preponderously in any direction. Of course it can *do* all these things, but it mustn't *look* as though it does, unless that happens to be the ideal of the day. The car has progressed through all sorts of idealised shapes and dimensions and probably the only golden rule of car design is that, whatever else it might look like, it mustn't appear to offer too much of an obstacle to forward movement. On the contrary, it must appear to be moving even when it's at rest.

In his mind's eye, the designer sees something that looks like an aeroplane fuselage or the hull of a yacht, or perhaps just a mathematically pure triangular wedge or an aero-spatial metal teardrop. To this shape has to be added a passenger compartment, a luggage compartment, an engine compartment and four wheels. All these features have to be moulded in a way that is organic to the desired shape of the thing. Moreoover, the thing has to resemble a car. It must be a continuation of all the cars that have come before; not just an *ad hoc* assembly of all the elements that comprise a car grafted on to some sort of fantastic or even scientifically plausible model of pure and effortless motion.

This much, in effect, is simple. But it's no use just designing a beautiful, emblematic, balanced and even functional object. It has to appeal on many other levels besides that of a piece of fanciful sculpture. Assuming it's not a luxury limousine or an exclusive sports car, there will be more important criteria.

If it's a saloon, for instance, it must remind a man that he can still cut a youthful and virile figure, but not to such an extent that his wife will recognise a threat to the marriage. If it's a modest coupé or an economy runabout, it must possess enough machismo to satisfy a young male purchaser but it mustn't be so bullish as to deter the potential female customer. Conversely, it

must be small, uncomplicated and practical enough to appeal to a busy woman but not so dainty as to emasculate a male driver. The neatest solution to the problem of a diverse market whose constituents wish to signal a great many different and variously shaded meanings to their fellows is called *trim*.

Trim cannot answer the demands made of engineering, however. A car must seem bigger inside than it appears outside. It must be fast, but it must also be safe. It must give a smooth, insulated ride, but it must also have firm, sensitive steering. These are problems of engineering design, but they are under the bonnet, out of sight. Uppermost in the buyer's mind is the question *Will I look good in it?* Or, since none of us is quite so openly vain, *Does it suit me?* This is a handy euphemism that also includes *Will it carry the children/shopping/golf clubs?* and *What will my wife/boss/neighbours/friends think?*

Providing the manufacturer has come up with a basically viable design, i.e., one that isn't square when the fashion is round, and presuming he is aiming at a particular section of the market, since no car can be a saloon, sports coupé and economy runabout at once (now there would be a design coup!) the next thing he must do is offer a variety of trim. The same engine can be bored out to two or three different sizes, with perhaps a better carburettor and improved suspension on the top model. Different interior fittings, optional extras, a whole spectrum of paint finishes and a galaxy of chrome and plastic grilles, bumpers, strips, badges, etc serve to distance the basic car from its progressively more costly relations.

By changing the trim from year to year as well as from car to car, the manufacturer can parade virtually a whole new range each year. The desirability of a new car, and thus the profitability of the industry, is enhanced when everyone can identify (and point and stare and mock) last year's model. In America, at the height of the frenzy, this yearly change was the rule, with a complete retooling for a new design every three to five years. In Europe, which couldn't support such rampant consumption, the time lapse tended to be longer: three to five years between changes of trim and ten to fifteen between new designs. As the industry becomes more rationalised and multinational, the trend is towards an international norm nearer the European level.

At its most innocent, this technique of standardised variety offers a reminder of the bespoke motoring style of the early part of the century. It is possible to own a custom-made automobile, a reflection of individual taste that is slightly apart from numerous other similar

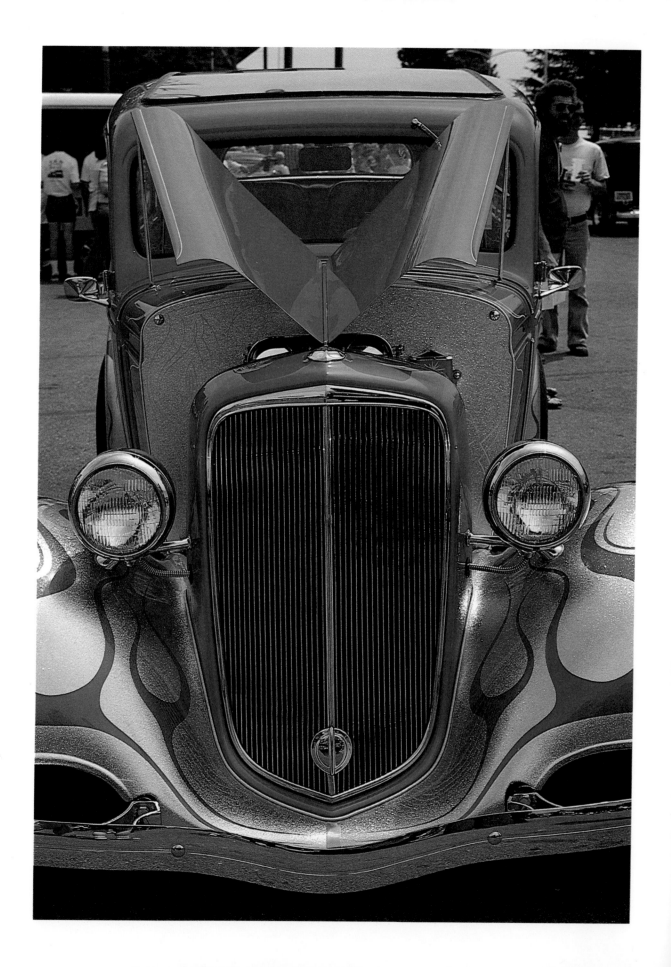

A customised thirties Ford.

Changes in car styling occurred rapidly by the late thirties. It was as if the molecules of a vintage car had been put into flux, causing the body to spread and merge with its ancillary wings, lights and bumpers. *Above left:* A 1940 Ford. *Above right:* A 1934 Ford. *Below:* A 1940 Chevrolet Sedan.

reflections of individual taste. But it is as a pointer of status that the sales trick works best. The glamour of the prestige model rubs off on the rest of the line. The same basic car comes in a host of guises; an economy compact can be a cheerful, dainty, feminine car in one, a dark, sporty bachelor transport in another. A popular joke about the Model T Ford was that it was available in any colour you wanted so long as it was black. But the marriage of marketing and design was just around the bend.

Ford retired the utilitarian Model T in 1927. Chrysler produced their one millionth Plymouth in 1934; it was available with a four- or six-cylinder engine and there were 258 combinations of bodywork and colour that could be specified on the same 107-inch chassis. The latest of the many teeming offspring of this unplanned but fortuitous, and ever more sophisticated, union has been the so-called 'world car' – a unit that can be constructed and sold worldwide under national marques with slight but sufficient variations in trim, and replaced after six to eight years with another unit boasting improved mechanics and a new look.

One of the first things the hot-rodders of the early 1950s did when they got hold of a '32 flathead Ford – an old car, discarded, proscribed, stigmatised, though evidently still with a few miles left in it – was to remove all the bumpers and the mudguards, the fenders and wheel arches and antiquated running-boards, all the chrome ornamentation that it acquired in its short life, all the extraneous clutter that surrounded the pure shape. A brazen, rebellious snub to Detroit? Probably not. They just wanted to make it go faster; as much by means of sympathetic magic as by weight reduction. With the trim and the fenders removed, the cockpit left open and the exhaust pipes exposed, the car took on the look of a pre-war racer. Here was a notion the manufacturers were just beginning to discover: that speed sometimes is as speed looks.

It will be obvious that the averages which go into the making of a volume production car entail a certain standard of mediocrity. As the industry dwindles to a handful of giants competing for the same mass markets, this is bound to be ever more the case.

Only the specialist manufacturer can afford to risk a startling, original design, partly in the hope that its very uniqueness will help it to sell; if it does, this will often influence the future shape of the volume car. It's a safe bet that the Porsche 928, with its bumperless front and rear impact zones, and the Giugiaro-designed Lotus

Esprit, (one of the lowest road cars ever made), both less than five years old, are future classics – just as every car that ever bore the prancing stallion of Ferrari is certain to be admired as long as there are roads left to drive them on.

There is something about a sports car, from the real boy racers to the mere toy racers, that few people can honestly resist . . . Not Isadora Duncan, who came out of her hotel in Nice on a warm September evening, wrapped a long scarf twice around her neck, and stepped into a brand new Bugatti tourer for a test drive along the Promenade des Anglais from which she would never return. Not James Dean, who had been itching for months to get out and race the silver 1500 four-cam Porsche Spyder that MGM had contractually forbidden him from driving while he was making *Giant*. The car was almost new, and another 200 miles on the clock before the race at Fresno would do it no harm at all. But Dean, his mechanic and the car would get no farther than the Sacramento turn-off . . .

Despite, or perhaps because of, this black lore, in addition to its already formidable infamy on the racing circuit, the sports car remains an alluring creation. Its pureness of form, like the grand contours of a true

By the late thirties, variations in trim turned one basic car into a whole range. This 1941 Chevy has had its hood (bonnet) and door trim removed, making it impossible to tell without looking inside whether it's a Special or a Deluxe.

luxury car, immediately distinguish it from more mundane transports. The sports car and the luxury car are exclusive, exotic creations, made in relatively small numbers to a higher mechanical standard, and destined to be prized, praised and preserved for these same reasons. It's estimated that over half of the 3-litre Bentleys made between 1921 and 1931 and seen as the epitome of the vintage era are still running today. But what of the Hudson Terraplane, or the Austin Atlantic, or the many other distinctive but workaday motor cars? What makes a custom classic? Why are some cars venerated for their exotic or bygone shape and others left to the inglorious fate of all metal?

Oddly enough, it's not the cars that were the pinnacle of the style of a particular period that are destined for nostalgic revival. Often these cars were not such popular sellers in their time as their more sedate counterparts. The relative sobriety of mass taste meant that the manufacturer had to soften the high fashion line in order to adjust to the times. Therefore, quite simply, there are fewer such cars around to be revived. They are, of course, more highly prized for their rarity and for their consummate expression of the style – a '59 Cadillac Eldorado Biarritz convertible will

be more emotive than a '57 Ford Fairlane – but they are beyond the means of the many amateurs in the field of automobile conservation.

During the 1950s, it was the V8 flathead Ford of 1932–36 that was most often selected for redemption by the growing teenage hot-rod sub-culture. Other cars of similar and even purer line could have been chosen, but might have presented the problem of parts and spares. The 1930s Ford was cheap and available. It was one of the biggest sellers of its day and so, twenty years later, there were still enough of them around to cannibalise.

The roadsters of the 1930s, however, were the first killers of the 'stocker' circuits, and their ranks grew thin as a result of the years of 'crash and burn' that paralleled the rock'n'roll era, leaving few to posterity. Like the '32 Ford, the 1955–57 Chevrolet also survived by virtue of numbers. It has become the car most readily identified with the 1950s, partly due to mythology, and partly to the fact that it was the biggest selling car of its day. No teenager could have been able to afford a new Chevy in 1956 (though they might have been able to borrow Dad's for a hot date) but within twenty years the car would become the

The Chrysler 'Airflow', designed by Chrysler's chief engineer Carl Breen, was an early attempt at aerodynamic styling. Introduced in 1934, it boasted several mechanical advancements as well as a shape that had benefited from six years in a wind tunnel. Admired by engineers but ridiculed by the public, its rounded, sloped body was a radical innovation compared to the upright square shape of its contemporaries. The Airflow was possibly the first of the futuristic dream cars, although it was nevertheless ignored by the buying public.

The status-enhancing quality of chrome. *Above:* A 1941 Cadillac, heralding the arrival of the horizontal grille. This was a unique step forward in car design that was to shape American grilles for the next fifteen years. *Below:* A 1946 Ford Super Deluxe.

The first post-war Cadillac, produced in 1947 from a 1942 design, but already bearing some of the pomp of victory.

A 1947 Plymouth Special, even with its stylish grille, was considered more of a spacious family saloon than a trend-setter.

mainstay of a 1950s revival.

The economic, technological, social and aesthetic influences on the size, shape and power of the automobile are too large to chronicle. There have been cars that have caught the public imagination and expressed the ideals of their time, cars that have fulfilled the practical needs of their age, and cars that have failed, however wondrously, to do either. Cars come to be treasured because they are unique and exclusive, like a Cord 812 or a Lamborghini Countach, or because they are typical, plentiful and familiar enough to become part of the common experience.

The Model T Ford served the needs of its time by being simply an affordable car. America has not since been renowned for producing utilitarian transport. One or two manufacturers tried. Powel Crossley spent $3 million in a rash attempt to introduce a small, cheap and, frankly, ugly car to the American public – who successfully resisted the idea until finally forced to swallow it by the actions of certain Middle Eastern states. The viability of Henry Ford's idea has been proven time and again, however, by such cars as the Ford Popular and the Austin Seven in Britain, the Fiat 508C Balilla in Italy, the Citroen 2CV in France, and the Volkswagen Beetle, designed by Ferdinand

Porsche on the orders of Chancellor Hitler and destined to be the biggest selling car of all time.

The Beetle is the perfect refutation of the Detroit marketing philosophy of annual updates and planned obsolescence. A design of the 1930s that sold well into the 1970s, it was only retired because the engine had been exhausted with improvement and by the 1970s was under-powered and outdated. Ironically, the Beetle almost survived long enough, through all the years of slabs, boxes and wedges, to see its stable aerodynamic curves come back into vogue. The Volkswagen was the inheritor of the virtues of the Model T; its name in fact means 'people's car'. To find its successor is the goal of the transnational giants in their search for a 'world car' – it's ultimately cheaper to produce the same car for thirty years than to produce a new car every six years.

But by their very nature, such cars only occur once in a generation, and they become, ultimately, part of the folklore of that generation. John Steinbeck looked back on this in *Cannery Row*: 'Two generations of Americans knew more about the Ford coil than the clitoris, more about the planetary system of gears than the solar system of stars ... Most of the babies of the period were conceived in the Model T Ford, and not a few were born in them. The theory of the Anglo-Saxon home became so warped that it never quite

Above: A 1939 Buick with continental kit.

37

Left to right: A customised
1932 Ford; a 1936 Ford Club
Sedan with continental kit and
tail lights that are unusually

styled; a 1947 Ford Club
Sedan; a 1948 Ford Super
Deluxe Convertible.

recovered.'

Henry Ford was thus the father of automobility (and perhaps the godfather of its accidental results) but he cannot similarly be held to account for the automania of subsequent generations. The Model T, remember, was available in any colour so long as it was black because only black enamel would dry fast enough. Duco lacquer had been introduced with the 'true blue' of the 1924 Oakland and it made possible mass-produced cars of all shades and colours. The Model T, like the Beetle, ultimately became mechanically rather than conceptually obsolete; but by 1927 buyers were demanding something grander than mere transportation when, for the first time, there were more people replacing their old car than buying their first.

This statistic was probably lost on William Crapo Durant, the great speculator and founder of General Motors, who once bought an uncertain refrigerator company for $56,000 on the grounds that a fridge was also a case with a motor (he named the company Frigidaire), and who clung to the opinion that the market for new cars would only be saturated 'when they quit making babies'. True or not, the company he founded, which rapidly became one of the twin giants of the automobile industry, took this idea to a place deep in its corporate heart. Alfred P. Sloan, Durant's successor as president of General Motors, who was described as 'the industry's first grey man', recalls in his autobiography that the policy of the 'annual model' instituted in the late 1920s was designed deliberately 'to create demand for the new value and, so to speak, create a certain amount of dissatisfaction with past models as compared with the new one'.

By the 1940s, the rationale was being more closely inspected. Psychologist Ernest Dichter divined that a man looks on a convertible as his mistress and on a saloon as his wife. Motivational research would soon have a small office along the corridor from the design department; its brief, to dig up the sub-conscious impulses of buyers. It revealed, not unexpectedly, that the motor car confirmed virility and was a way of compensating for growing old. It isolated and quantified what Vance Packard called 'the upgrading urge', a strong motivator in the new automobile suburbs, where people bought a car they couldn't afford to show other people they could afford it. All this information quickly found its way to the advertising department, where it soon caused E. B. White of *The New Yorker* to complain: 'From reading the auto ads you would think that the primary function of the motor car in America was to carry its owner first into a higher social stratum, and then into an exquisite delirium of high adventure.'

Henry Ford, a rational man, held out against it as long as he could, which was about as long as it took Chevrolet (GM's major division) to surpass Ford's annual sales. This happened in 1927 and it was, as near as can be found, the beginning of automania; wherein the motor car exceeds its prosaic function and becomes a piece of figurative sculpture, an anonymous but powerful work of art to be, in Roland Barthes' phrase, 'consumed in image by a whole population'.

Barthes was writing in *Les Lettres Nouvelles* about the first public showings in 1955 of the Citroën DS, a remarkable new design to replace the twenty-year-old Traction-Avant. With its headlights set like eyes on bulging wings, and a long, supine bonnet tracing a near-perfect ellipse, the DS resembled a giant metal toad crouching for a leap. Panels hid the rear wheels and gave the impression, when the lowest of its hydro-pneumatic ride positions was selected, that the car was hovering on the road like a flying saucer. Barthes, in fact, thought it obvious that the new Citroën had fallen from the sky 'inasmuch as it appears at first sight as a superlative *object*'.

Barthes was impressed with the paradoxical lightness and bulk of the design: 'Speed is here expressed by less aggressive, less athletic signs, as if it were evolving from a primitive to a classical form.' He describes the windows as 'vast walls of air and space, with the curvature, the spread, and the brilliance of soap bubbles'. The dashboard, he concluded, was 'more like the working surface of a modern kitchen than the control room of a factory'.

It had taken a long time to arrive at this plastic chapel of a benevolent technology. The exterior of the American car evolved steadily with each consecutive model change, vintage proportions slowly giving way to the streamline. Separate wings and headlights grew into the body. Drop-frame construction did away with running boards, except as a cosmetic touch, and brought the rear wheels under the body of the car instead of protruding either side. It was as if the molecules of a vintage car had been put into flux, melting the tall square box of the roof line, and causing the body to spread and merge with its ancillary wings, lights and bumpers. The long, straight bonnet of the vintage shape, with the radiator grille rising flat and vertical over the front axle and a gentle arch spreading back on top to the windscreen, was gradually softened almost by the force of the wind of years of driving. V-

The 1941 Cadillac tail light; by 1948 it would have evolved into the embryo tail fin.

Preceding pages: Polished examples of a Ford V6 (*above*), Rover (Buick) V8 (*below*), and Jaguar V12 (*right*).
Above: A new wing detail from a 1946 Buick and (*below*) the front grille.

shaped radiator grilles and swept tails began to appear, offering a leading edge to the churning air. Headlights moved out on to the wings. The nose grew rounder and began to extend prow-like over the front axle, allowing the passenger compartment to begin one-third instead of half-way along the body length.

By 1940, with the war about to cause a long-lasting divergence of the transatlantic line, the motor car had acquired the style of a building by Frank Lloyd Wright. Speed was emphasised by thin horizontal fluting, the decorative detail that was repeated throughout the architecture of the day. Everything about the car was fluid and curved, with bodies that swept like a bow around to the bulging rear – an echo, perhaps, of the tight-waisted rump and accentuated calves of women's fashion.

Chrysler made an early attempt in 1934 at mathematical as opposed to merely stylistic aero-dynamics with their Chrysler and De Soto Airflow models – the result, it was claimed, of six years in a wind tunnel. Despite its low silhouette, the car *looked* rather ponderous and failed to catch on. Its production ceased in 1937, but a more elegant and flowing version of the style would become the norm within a few years.

By the start of the 1940s, American cars were lower, longer, broader and more massive than ever before. Grilles were wider, bumpers heavier, and the ideal line was drawn with an ever greater flourish. The front wings on GM cars now ended in the middle of the front doors. Function had been sacrificed to form.

On February 9th, 1942, the war brought car design to a temporary halt. When production resumed in the summer of 1945, it was estimated that the automobile industry had contributed more material to the Allied effort than any other. In addition to all the scout cars, armoured cars and carriers, it contributed eighty-five per cent of the steel helmets, seventy-five per cent of the aircraft engines, and fifty-seven per cent of the tanks. In Germany, the preparations for war had also brought about the building of the world's first national motorway network.

For the remainder of the decade, the American public was offered mainly pre-war designs, so it wasn't until the 1950s that the car style wars could be resumed in earnest. In December of 1951, the hundred millionth passenger car built in the US took to the road. It was, if anything, even bigger than before. The bonnet and front wings had become integrated, with just a slight central hump to recall their once separate functions of covering the engine and the front wheels. The radiator grille was no longer perpendicular to the road but now spread across the width of the car and merged with the front bumper. The passenger cell now ended at the rear axle, and the boot (or trunk) instead of rolling grandly down with the curve of the roof and the rear wheel arch, tended to reflect the line of the bonnet, with a flat deck curving briskly down to the rear bumper and the rear wheels often vanishing underneath.

Throughout the 1950s and into the 1960s these dimensions were extended and straightened and squared into the familiar three-box shape which, since there is nothing so unfashionable as that which has just gone out of fashion, is now almost universally shunned. After a brief flurry of angular, wedge-shaped designs, the recent reminder of finite resources is creating a move (back) towards softer and more rounded shapes. A close look at almost all new cars that are not built to Japanese or American taste will reveal that what appears at first sight to be a straight line is usually very slightly bowed or rounded. It has been found that air, which is not subject to the vicissitudes of style, will always flow more smoothly around a curve than around a rectangle.

Until now, only the designers of sports and racing

A 1946 Buick: detail of dashboard.

A 1953 Cadillac Fleetwood
Series 75.

A twenties Brewster, possibly the first custom car, with its distinctive heart-shaped grille, coach built and designed by the firm of Brewster on a standard Ford Model T chassis.

cars have been constrained by such details as drag coefficient. All the rest were free to pursue their own fanciful routes towards stylistic motion and whatever else needed to be said in metal at the time. In America in the 1950s, when the industry reached a peak of technological and styling extravagance, there was manifestly a great deal to be said. The motor car, which had by then become endemic to the American way of life, was to be its most voluble expression.

European and American styling diverged in the immediate post-war years and, while influences continued to pass to and fro, the demands of the respective markets have only recently begun to be reconciled. The European, primarily Italian, ideal was sleek and restrained. It took shape from the influential Cisitalia coupé of 1947 with bodywork by G.B. Pininfarina, a car now preserved in New York's Museum of Modern Art as one of 'the eight most important cars in the world'. The following year, Cadillac (General Motors' prestige division) introduced their first new post-war design. Rising in a pleasing little hump on the rear wings was an unusual tail light treatment. It was to be the first of many squadrons of tail fins.

The '48 Cadillac was designed by Bill Mitchell, Frank Hershey, Art Ross and Harley Earl, working as part of Earl's Art and Colour Studio at GM, and it was based, fancifully enough, on the Lockheed P-38 Lightning pursuit fighter. 'During the war,' wrote Alfred Sloan, 'an Air Force friend of Harley Earl had invited him to see some new fighter planes. One of them was the P-38, which had twin Allison engines, twin fuselages, and twin tail fins. When Mr Earl saw it he asked if he could have some of his designers look at it ...' The drama and mystique of this piece of American technological supremacy had a profound effect on Earl and his team. Their sketches began to echo the features of the airplane: fuselage profiles, pontoon wings, cockpit-like windows, over-riders shaped like nose cones and rising tail fins.

The tail fin caught on, reckoned Harley Earl (rather ingenuously) because it gave owners 'an extra receipt for their money in the form of a visible prestige marking for an expensive car'. Bill Mitchell had a simpler explanation: 'From a design standpoint, the fins gave definition to the rear of the car for the first time. They made the back end as interesting as the front.' By 1959, a car without a tail fin was a car without wheels. Cadillac had the tallest, a full three feet and six inches above the ground. Chrysler, however, had the most implausible excuse: 'Sweeping finned lines, pioneered by cars of the Forward Look, aren't just for looks!' So blushed an ad for the '59 De Soto. 'Based on aerodynamic principles, they make a

Above left: A 1940 Ford Sedan Delivery. *Above right:* The 1940 Packard was a popular car with the rich and fashionable, outselling the Cadillac. This model has been revised with an elegant upright front with side grilles.

49

A 1939 Buick, sporting an
aerodynamic and streamlined
grille.

Above: A 1941 Lincoln-Zephyr, designed by John Tjaarda. *Below:* A 1942 Lincoln-Zephyr, with a restyled front. An optional extra was the Liquamatic Drive automatic gear shift.

A 1947 Packard Super
Clipper Touring Sedan, sold
for $2149.

Above: Ten body types were available on this 1948 Ford Super Deluxe model. *Below:* A 1947 Mercury Town Sedan.

real contribution to the remarkable stability of these cars on the road.'

Besides the '48 Cadillac, the aircraft influence was also discernible on several of its contemporaries. The '49 Oldsmobile Futuramic, another post-war design from Earl's GM studio, wore headlights set in miniature aircraft engine air scoops. The same year, the first new post-war Ford design featured an unashamedly symbolic and quite sizeable chrome model aircraft nose and wings in place of what was once just a grille to protect the radiator.

But wartime engineering had a more important effect under the bonnet than outside it with the introduction by Cadillac and Oldsmobile in 1949 of the lightweight, high-compression, high-rev ohv V8 engine, designed to take advantage of anticipated high-octane fuel. The Cadillac engine was ten per cent more powerful and nearly 200lbs lighter than its predecessor. Installed in the smaller models of the range, which were still large, heavy cars, it could deliver a 0–60 mph time of thirteen seconds and easily reach 100 mph. A 1950 Cadillac finished tenth at Le Mans that year – a fine showing for a luxury car. Its speed down the Mulsanne straight was as high as 120 mph. Edward Gaylord, an amateur racer of the time, owned a 1950 Sedanet with manual transmission and a 3.77 axle ratio, and also one of the new Jaguar XK-120s. 'The Cadillac was the faster car up to about 90 mph,' he recalls. 'My Cadillac set what was then a stock car record at the original quarter-mile drag races in Santa Ana, California ... The only competition I had was from the small 135-hp Oldsmobile 88 coupé.'

Oldsmobile put their V8 – developed separately in an inter-divisional contest at GM – into the short-wheelbase Rocket 88 which, though the company did not sponsor racing, rapidly became a circuit favourite. Of the nine NASCAR Grand National events in 1949, the Rocket 88 won six. It was immortalised by blues shouter Jackie Brenston in his pounding, frantic *Rocket 8-88*, recorded by Sam Phillips for the Chess label in 1951 and cited by many as the first rock'n'roll record.

Its reputation as a 'hot' car thus assured, the Rocket 88 went on to become a motorhead favourite of the early 1950s. It was challenged in 1953 by the Hudson Hornet, and then in 1955 by the new Chevrolet V8. Designed by Ed Cole, who also built the Cadillac V8, the '55 Chevy 265-ci V8 was a milestone engine. In 1957, in its bored-out, fuel-injected 283-ci form it became the first mass-production engine to deliver one horse-power per cubic inch (the US engine size measurement), and its descendants still power many modern cars.

Just as war technology had liberated the American car – by creating the power necessary to move it – so war bucks would let loose its consumers. In 1950, car ownership in America reached the 50 million mark; ten years later the figure was 75 million. The deprivations of the war – when Americans had been starved of the opportunity to buy new cars – were now over and life had resumed with a new vigour. In a country so vast and sprawling, the motor car is vital, but the car of the 1950s was as much a product of glory as necessity. With their V8 engines coupled to more efficient automatic transmission, and the new torsion-bar suspension, these cars could do what glory demanded.

Come the late 1950s, America – if the automobile is any indication – was well into its baroque period. Chromium had first replaced nickel-plating on some 1925 models, and it was now being applied in huge decorative stucco scoopfuls. The front end of the American car acquired a frightful grimace: grilles snarled like sharks, and bumpers jutted out like the square jaws of a super-patriot. Lewd bullet-shaped projectiles mimicked the idealised female figure of the time and were nicknamed 'Dagmars' after a starlet whose contribution to the screen has sadly not survived her contribution to popular mythology. Aircraft symbolism ran riot until finally out-and-out science fiction, which had a mysterious grip on the late 1950s' imagination, took over as the prime source of inspiration.

The fantastic styling that evolved in that decade was obviously not the result of engineering logic. American cars may have looked 'aerodynamic' but in fact the most mathematical body of the time, other than those of some sports cars, belonged to the Citroën DS. The archetypal American shape of the 1950s was really just a draughtboard dream, reflecting the naivety of an age now fondly remembered for just that. Chrome-encrusted Pan-American liners like the Cadillac, outlandish rococco roadsters like the Mercury Turnpike Cruiser, and aerospace fantasies like the Plymouth Fury have all been consigned along with other 1950s breakthroughs, such as push-button gear-change and vacuum ashtrays, to automotive limbo. It was a time when people craved strange symbols of luxury and status, and could seriously aspire to be seen riding around in a mass-produced two-and-a-half ton salmon pink steel space rocket.

Above: A 1952 Pontiac Chieftain Eight, with a sun visor. Stylistically this car has not changed from the 1951 model, but dual-range Hydra-Matic Drive Transmission was now an optional extra with the high-compression engines.
Below: The 1953 Packard Patrician 400 was mounted on a 127 wheelbase and powered by a 327 engine which could reach 155 hp.

The 1958 Cadillac Coupe DeVille must surely be the pinnacle of the late fifties' car design. The extraordinary rear fins, rubber-tipped bumpers, double headlights and tail lights added the finishing touches to this daring car.

These cars were the opposite of the carefully costed and market researched committee cars of today. Back in the 1930s, Alfred Sloan had learned from fledgling GM research that the public ranked styling first; automatic transmission second; and high-compression engines third – in other words looks, convenience and speed respectively – in their choice of which car to buy. Styling, therefore, became the main priority and Harley J. Earl was put in charge. He used to tell his stylists: 'Go all the way, then back off.'

To best see what 'all the way' might look like, a scale model moulded in clay on a wooden frame would be built first, and then finally a real car on a rolling chassis. It made sense, at this stage, to gauge public reaction by exhibiting the prototype, rather than tooling up for a car that nobody would want to buy. The demands of the annual model meant that risks had to be taken, changes had to be made, new styles introduced, but not at the cost of alienation. Here, as it turned out, was an effective way to court desire.

GM tried it in 1933 at the Chicago World's Fair with the Cadillac Aerodynamic. The car had what was then considered a very sophisticated line; though not aerodynamic in its later sense, it drew admiring crowds. In 1939, Harley Earl's team produced an unusually smooth and low-slung roadster called the Buick 'Y' with an electric hood and retractable headlights. It was exhibited at the New York World's Fair as part of GM's Futurama – a building designed by Bel Geddes and devoted to what motorised America might look like in 1960. An overhead carousel ferried visitors across a gigantic working model of an automated highway built for safe and effortless speed, and on into the city of the future, with raised walkways for pedestrians and free-flowing traffic beneath. Turning a corner, the carousel deposited visitors in a full-size mock-up of the downtown intersection they had just seen, filled, naturally, with all the latest GM models.

In 1941, Chrysler responded as best they could to this promotional coup with the Thunderbolt, a superb creation by Le Baron with enclosed wheels, retractable headlights, and electric windows and door locks. Whereas GM had restricted themselves to predicting the environment, the Thunderbolt was a deliberate piece of futurism. It was touted as a car you might, one far-off day, be able to buy (one day when all cities might look like Fritz Lang's *Metropolis*), of which six examples were built for display by Chrysler dealers.

What began as an 'idea car' had now become a 'show car' and it wasn't long before it would be a 'dream car' – a flight of the stylist's fancy that was exhibited alongside the latest models and would inspire, with its emphasis on novelty and change, a decade of unchecked neomania. 'The reactions of hundreds of thousands of viewers to these so-called dream cars,' said Alfred Sloan, in a piece of typical corporate bluff, 'showed that the public wanted and was ready to accept more daring steps in styling and engineering.' George Walker, Ford vice-president in charge of styling, put it more like a true car salesman: 'These dream cars aren't as futuristic as they look. Stick around for a year or two and we'll prove it.'

Sometimes, though not often, the cars were mechanically as well as stylistically innovative. The Buick XP-300 of 1951 took engineer Charles Payne four years to develop. Among its many new features was a super-charged 335-hp 3.5 litre V8 that burned petrol below 2,500 rpm and methanol at higher revs, producing a 0-60 mph figure of only eight miniscule seconds. More common were cars like Harley Earl's Buick Le Sabre, produced two years previously and based on the new F-86 Sabre jet fighter – a car which would influence stylists and customisers for years to come. It had a wrap-around windscreen, tail lights set on tall fins and exhaust outlets incorporated in the rear bumper, details that would be commonplace by the end of the decade.

Earl actually used the Le Sabre on the road for several years, and many of GM's show cars were driveable, if not always produceable, vehicles. The same was true of the Chrysler specials styled by Virgil Exner. Ford, however, contented themselves with mock-ups. In view of the fact that Ford came up with the wildest ideas of all, incorporating gyro-stabilisers, video display, push-button steering, and 'compact nuclear propulsion devices', this was perhaps to be expected.

The Buick Le Sabre was exhibited at the first GM Motorama of 1949, where it stole the limelight from the conventional new models and persuaded the company of the viability of incorporating some of its features in later designs. The car itself was never offered for sale, unlike the Chevrolet Corvette, a 1953 dream car which was such a hit that it immediately went into production.

The Motoramas also spawned the Autoramas, sponsored by dealers in the smaller cities. A young visitor to an Autorama in the mid 1950s was Chip Lord: 'All I can remember is that the cars under those bright lights had a sculptural glamour and desirability that in me inspired hysteria. In retrospect I know they were art – stationary objects in a museum-like environment – but I've never gotten that kind of a rush from a real museum.'

Opposite: A 1958 Cadillac Coupe DeVille. *Above left:* Detail of front grille with rubber tips and double headlights. *Above right:* One of Cadillac's most extreme tail fins. *Below:* An elegant side profile.

The styling eccentricities of the late fifties were tested on the public via a series of 'dream cars' exhibited at the auto-fairs. *Above:* Designed by Le Baron, only six Chrysler Thunderbolts were ever manufactured. Among the many details on the car were push button controls, including door locks and electric windows, as well as the retractable headlights and roof. *Below:* Harley Earl in his immediately successful 1951 Buick Le Sabre, a car that sported many features that would later be transposed onto production models. Influenced by contemporary aircraft styling, design details included headlights concealed behind a rotating central panel, and twin exhausts set into the tail fin below the three tail lights. The body panels were cast in magnesium and a rain sensitive panel, set between the heated seats, would automatically raise the hood.

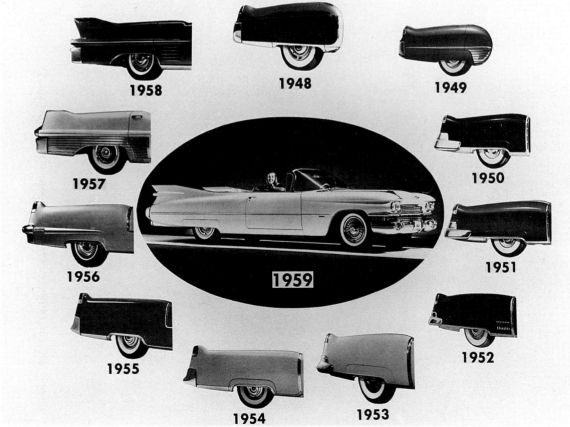

1958 1948 1949

1957 1950

1956 1951

1959

1955 1954 1953 1952

The Ford design studio
succeeded in dreaming up the
most fanciful cars, although
their creations didn't always
get past the clay model stage.
Above: A 1954 FX-Atmos
Ford, which startled the 1954
Chicago Auto Show.
According to the vice-
President of Ford, its purpose
was to 'represent one of the
many avenues which styling
could take in the future'.
Below: A 1959 publicity shot
for Chevrolet.

CHAPTER 3

FORGIVE THEM DEAR FORD

Chip Lord finally lost his innocence – not in the back seat of a mythical Chevrolet, but on the campus of an American university in the late 1960s. Writing in *Automerica*, he doesn't even pause to recount the events that disabused him of his youthful automotive dreams – as first Vietnam and then the gas crisis forced a reappraisal of the ethos behind the American car. But the book goes on to record a wistful tribute paid to the faded and ruined ideals of the car culture called the Cadillac Ranch.

Created by Lord and other members of the Ant Farm collective, the Cadillac Ranch is a series of ten Cadillacs planted nose down, tail fins in the air, in the flat Texas farmland alongside Route 66. It s an obvious and amusing statement; a moving piece of irony made from old pieces of moving iron, a kind of Dinosaur Park of the 1950s car. It also marks, perhaps, the final stage of a long and spectacular evolution. 'The car as vehicle,' wrote Marshall McLuhan, 'will go the way of the horse. The horse has lost its role in transportation but has made a strong comeback in entertainment.'

The car, indeed, has always been strong in entertainment, but here McLuhan is predicting a change from activity to spectacle. The days of the car as recreation and even necessity are numbered, he suggests, by a television-induced immobility (let alone by the then unforeseen energy shortage). Goods would still travel by road, but not people. No longer would suburban Sundays echo to the clang of spanner on asphalt. The motor car will have come a hundred thousand million miles, only to arrive as the central figure of a new genre of popular fiction; the exploits it gave rise to chronicled as myth, the landscape it shaped recreated in a twenty-first-century version of John Ford's Monument Valley.

While McLuhan might well, in the long run, be right . – and it's now possible to predict a time when computer technology will enable TV to supplant the car as the principal means of social interaction – there are two important facets of automobility, the motorised lifestyle, that will be hard to surrender. One is that the car enables young people to escape from the home, which is something they will want to do as long as there are homes to escape from. The other is that the car is a toy that works: a big grown-up toy that goes fast and makes a lot of noise and has a lot of moving parts and looks, well ... it looks just *wonderful*.

Playing with this toy, pressing the buttons, operating the pedals, tinkering with it, seeing how it works, what it will do, enjoying the excitement of it in motion, washing it with a loving leather caress, getting bored with it (like all toys) and changing it; this is the stuff of a deep-rooted addiction. Add to it the powerful motivator of status – at first simply to own a car, a rite of passage into manhood, and then to own a faster, bigger, better, newer, shinier, grander one – and McLuhan's future begins to look glum, joyless, and lacking in what remains the greatest single tonic for ever more restless nerves.

No doubt some other means of signifying status would be found if and when the horseless age comes to an end. Doubtless, too, the urge for individual expression would find some other outlet. But for the time being, the car will have to serve. It is probably no chance result of industrial processes that the most brightly and variously coloured things in an average suburban street are the curtains at the windows, the flowers in the gardens, and the cars on the road.

The compulsion to decorate, to adorn, to be different (within the accepted boundaries) and to put this difference on display cannot even be thwarted by such homogeneous products as the world car. It's this compulsion that has yielded the most extreme and perhaps the most poignant manifestation of the car culture: the souped-up, resprayed, chopped, channelled and ever-changing automaniac world of the custom car fanatic and rod-o-holic.

It's worth distinguishing the two. While they might convene around the same cars, it might not be for the same reasons; a car that might appeal to one could just as easily appeal to the other.

The Mercedes 300SL, for instance, would have been prized by both. With a 240-bhp engine transporting it up to 150 mph, it was the fastest production car of 1955 and no hot-rodder could fail to be moved by this fact. The sleek, low, muscular body and the gullwing doors, hinged to swing upwards from the centre of the roof, were also enough to make any

Opposite: One of a series of ten Cadillacs planted nose down on Cadillac Ranch in Amarillo, Texas.

Two fifties-style hot rods. *Above:* This thirties V8 Ford Coupe has had its top chopped and the front windscreen reduced in height by a fairly modest amount, compared to some examples. The engine cowl, front fenders, badges and trim have all been removed. *Below:* Another thirties roadster, this one a rag top that has been lowered down on its chassis. The cowl remains, but it has been louvred, again the only detail on a body devoid of badges, trim and even door handles, as well as both front and rear fenders.

Radical hot rods. *Above:* This 1938 Ford is a near original, apart from a drastic increase in height achieved by jacking the suspension to make way for outsize wheels. *Below:* An eccentric treatment to the front end of a standard thirties roadster.

Drag racing at Orange County Raceway. Since it's impossible to tell what engine they're running under the bonnet, the outward vintage of these cars gives no indication of their performance. As a result, what seems like a remarkably well-preserved twenties Model T might easily out-race a car fifty years younger. *Above:* A 1941 Willys: The original Gasser. *Opposite:* A 1940 Mercury, chopped and channelled.

customiser's eyes pop. But the 300SL was a European car, exotic, refined and expensive; not a car to which you could cheerfully take a wrench or a blow torch on an idle weekend. Yet it didn't come off the peg from Detroit, so if anyone else wanted to own one, that was okay.

A more suitable vehicle for the respective fantasies of hot-rodders and customisers of the late 1950s would be a '51 Chrysler Saratoga. Now, here there was room for improvement. With some modifications to the cam shaft, carbs and exhaust manifold, the Chrysler hemi-head V8 could be pushed up to over 300 bhp. So long as there were no Rocket 88s, Hudson Hornets or Chevy V8s around to argue, you had yourself a pretty fair contender in any stock car contest. It didn't look like much – in fact it was downright ugly – but it was fast, and this to a true hot-rodder was the paramount virtue of any car.

It's a misapprehension to think of the hot-rodder as the owner of a 1930s stripped-down highboy roadster, prone to anti-social behaviour and destined to cool his heels in reform school if not, after the inevitable high-speed spill, in the local morgue. The owner of the stripped-down highboy might equally be a customiser, not especially concerned about the power of the engine, but determined that the thing should look 'neat'.

Faced with the Chrysler Saratoga – and money being no object – he would chop the roof height by three or four inches, lower or 'channel' the body down over the wheels by about the same amount, and maybe alter the shape of the fenders at the same time, replace the door handles with hidden electric solenoids, remove all the trim and weld over the holes, 'french' the headlights and aerial, and lastly swap the bumpers, tail lights, hubcaps and grille for those of another car. After several deep, lustrous coats of trick paint had been applied, another radical custom would take, one imagines very gingerly, to the stunned and disconcerted roads.

In some respects, the hot-rodder and the customiser shared the same inspiration: speed was the quest of the hot-rodder, and its look the concern of most customisers. 'My primary purpose for twenty-eight years,' said Harley Earl in a *Saturday Evening Post* article of 1954, 'has been to lengthen and lower the American automobile, at times in reality and always at least in appearance.' The customiser inherited this ideal. Longer and lower was synonymous with faster and sleeker, as Earl well knew; the suggestion, or the look, of speed is often enough.

If it wasn't a crazy car or an extravagant charabanc that the customiser was after, it was a car that looked faster. All of the more credible (as opposed to

incredible) post-war customs sport features that can be traced to the race track; be it removing all the chrome and the fenders, louvring the bonnet, jacking the rear, adding fat tyres or, more recently, adding air foils and front spoilers. The net effect is to invoke speed by way of sympathetic magic. None of these alterations would make a car *go* very much faster – not without a long programme of testing and adjustment – but they are the paraphernalia of the fast car.

Fast cars, in Europe, are primarily the sport of the rich. In America, after the war, the sport was open to any hot-headed youth who wanted to participate, and participation could occur almost anywhere. Partly money, and partly tradition, made this so. Aside from those in Mexico, there were no established road races of the European sort, and since the collapse of the Cord-Duesenberg-Auburn company in 1935, there had been no US sports car makers of the likes of Lotus or Ferrari for whom a racing commitment was an essential part of their business. In fact, until the Chevrolet Corvette arrived in 1953, followed by the Ford Thunderbird in 1954, there were no US production sports cars.

Recognised races in America were confined to the

big oval circuit contests like the Indianapolis and Daytona 500s (over a distance of 500 miles) and to the many stocker tracks on which anything that could pass for a production car – the engines were often discreetly modified and always tuned up – could join in a madcap, careening, ricocheting eliminator.

American racing was largely an amateur affair. Industry involvement even in the prestigious 500s was scarce until the 1950s. So-called 'dirt-cars', racing cars scratch-built by either a small team or a lone competitor, were frequent winners at Indianapolis, the last being Troy Ruttman's Agajanian Special in 1952, which set a new track record average of 138.9 mph. The official US racing colours were jokingly held to be grey primer.

Perhaps the greatest arena of speed in America, was the speed trial on the flat. The country's natural geography, and not a few of its roads, offered the perfect opportunity for speed in a straight line – a race against the clock and the limits of mechanical tolerance. Since the turn of the century, places like Daytona beach in Florida, the Bonneville salt flats in Utah, and the California dry lakes had played host to small teams of engineers wheeling strange curvilinear

Two examples of the minimal aesthetic in customising. Both these fifties Chevrolets have had their massive chrome bumpers and much of the chrome hood (bonnet) trim removed. *Above:* A jacked up 1952 Chevy Deluxe Styleline.

monsters into position and gazing across the flat, shimmering horizon at the unknown edge of land-bound motion. Even Europeans who wanted a try were obliged to travel to these venues.

As befits American tradition, the stocker circuits and the speed trials, and even many of the 500s, were frontiers open to individuals and entrepreneurs. One such was Bill Kenz who, in partnership with Roy Leslie, created a hot-rod legend that spanned fifty years, from the occasional backroads duel in the 1920s to the huge commercial circus of drag racing in the 1970s.

Kenz and Leslie's celebrated twin-engined '777' streamliner left a ferocious trail across the hot-rod heyday, winning the *Hot Rod* magazine trophy for top speed five times between 1950 and '57. No doubt teenage hot-rodders of the time would have earned themselves an even worse reputation for public nuisance had they been able to figure out for themselves how to link the crankshafts of two flathead V8s.

Kenz, like the brothers Chevrolet before him, started out by making performance adjustments to the Model T. In Denver, where Kenz worked as a junior mechanic at a local Ford garage, the Model T tended to suffer from the high altitudes of the Rockies. Kenz began tinkering with the engines in search of improved power. As soon as he could afford a car of his own – a Model T, inevitably – he was ready to fit a Fronte-nac overhead conversion, aluminium pistons, Bosch ignition and Ruxtell two-speed transmission, raising the top speed of the car to 68 mph. It would do for a start.

By the time he acquired his third car, a '31 Ford Victoria, he had learned the knack of 'eyeball engineering'. With no hot-rod magazines to show him the way, and few after-market parts available, hopping up an engine was essentially a matter of experiment. Kenz tried reversing the cam in the Victoria's engine block, creating four intake ports and two exhausts instead of the other way around. This helped raise the Ford's top speed to nearly 100 mph, which must have come as a shock to anyone in Denver running an expensive Duesenberg roadster. Kenz raced the Victoria in some of the new stock car class races of the early 1930s at a paved track outside town.

With Roy Leslie as his partner, Bill Kenz opened his own garage. After a decade of informal racing and professional modifying, he decided during the slack

Above: A 1957 Chevy Bel Air with the bonnet seams welded.

The 1940 Mercury Coupe, the first of the Ford Mercurys and a favourite for this radical fifties-style custom job. The top has been chopped and the windscreen raked to lose an inch or so off the roof line, while the body has been channelled (dropped down over the chassis), leaving only minimal ground clearance. All the badges and trim have been removed and the seams have been welded, filled and painted over; even the door handles have been replaced by electric solenoids. A pair of moon discs on the front wheels complete the authentic appearance of this period custom.

Subjected to another radical custom job in the fifties style, this fifties Mercury has undergone a drastic top chop, as well as being channelled by as much as three inches. The headlights have been 'Frenched' – tunnelled back into the wings – and as usual the trim and badges have been removed and the seams welded. The original Mercury grille has been replaced with what looks like a 1953/5 Corvette grille.

In 1950, General Motors' Chevrolet series gave them the highest production volume of any auto manufacturer in history, selling 2,108,273 cars in one year. By December of that year they had produced their 25th million vehicle overall. *Above:* A 1950 Chevrolet Deluxe Styleline. Its body has been channelled slightiy and the headlights have been Frenched. *Below:* A 1954 Ford Crestline Convertible. The bonnet seams have been filled, the headlights Frenched and the original grille has been replaced by a row of ferocious teeth – in actuality a grille cannibalised from a 1953 DeSoto.

war years to build a rear-engined racer based on Ferdinand Porsche's Auto-Unions of the late 1930s but made with backyard genius out of Ford parts and a '32 pick-up truck. With the rear engine installed it seemed logical to add a second in front; if not logical at least possible with a trick clutch in between ... They were soon racing the pick-up on abandoned roads on the outskirts of town. 'We used to have some pretty good Sunday morning speed tests out there,' Kenz later told hot-rod historian Jay Storer. 'The hot roadsters of the day were running around 110–115 mph and the pick-up would run 125.'

In 1949, Kenz and Leslie got word on the growing hot-rod grapevine that a big speed trial was to be held at the Bonneville salt flats. *Hot Rod* magazine had started in 1948 and timing associations were being formed, patterned on the Southern California Timing Association (SCTA), to organise, supervise and quantify the backroad (and sometimes main road) sport of drag racing. Kenz and Leslie reasoned that they would have the drop on the dry lakes racers in that their engines were tuned for the higher altitudes of the Bonneville flats. The pick-up ran up to 141 mph, but more importantly, it introduced the pair to hundreds of hot-rodders from California who shared the same obsessions; a loose fraternity of backyard and workshop motorheads whose country had marshalled all the power of technology to win a war and who were now going to harness part of this power to contraptions that would slake their demon thirst for speed.

The Kenz and Leslie 777 streamliner arrived at Bonneville the following year. It was powered by two 200-hp Edelbrock-equipped flathead Fords and draped in a body of elemental aerodynamic proportions modelled on the So-Cal Special built by Alex Xydias and Dean Batchelor and powered by a single Edelbrock-built Ford Mercury engine that had been the fastest car at the flats in 1949. After some hasty alterations to the air intakes when it was found that the air was flowing so smoothly over the body that not enough of it was entering the carbs, the 777 surpassed its disappointing early speed of 168 mph and reached over 200 mph. 'Everybody on the salt was excited,' recalls Jay Storer. 'An American home-built hot-rod had exceeded the magic figure of 200 mph and might even go faster.' Eventually the car hit 210 mph, at which speed the treads suddenly ripped from the tyres. Its racing tyres were only good for speeds of up to 175 mph. Luckily, driver Willy Young was able to hold the car to a straight course. When the crew reached him, he wasn't too badly shaken, unlike his watch, which had rattled to pieces.

'Nobody invented hot-rodding,' said Wally Parks in 1962. 'It just happened.'

Parks was a founder member of the National Hot-Rod Association, formed in 1951 as an off-shoot of the SCTA. Throughout the US, but most of all in Southern California, there were people like Bill Kenz, giving cars a performance overhaul, making new parts and modifying old ones. Midwestern and eastern hop-up artists put their work on the track, but in the west they put theirs on the streets, where everyone could see and copy.

The weather was good in California, there was plenty of space to test the cars, and vehicle regulations were not so heavily enforced. So long as a car was not doing anything illegal, the lack of fenders was usually ignored. So, too, was the nose-down racing car look achieved by running Firestone 5×16 dirt or sprint car front tyres and slightly larger 7×16 rear ones. The car might be built for show or to go, but it was impossible to tell without looking under the bonnet, where, in virtually all of the rods except the real hot cars and nearly half of the customs, there would be a Ford V8, with or without the performance extras.

The perfect post-war rod was a late 1920s early 1930s rag-top roadster. The '32 Ford was the best. It needed no serious body alterations to achieve the ideal line, just a custom dash with Stewart Warner instruments to go with the custom upholstery and paint, removal of all trim right down to the door handles, hydraulic brakes from a later Ford, tail lights from either a '38 Ford or a '41 Chevy, Arrow Accessory sealed-beam headlights, some twin pipes running from a Belond, Douglass or Clark manifold, and perhaps a column gear shift to go with a Zephyr transmission that would squeeze a little more power from first and second.

Once this had 'just happened', in Wally Parks' phrase, who could tell what else might follow? By the mid 1950s, hot-rodders had acquired a notoriety second only to motorcycle gangs. They might descend at any time on a quiet Southern California township, racing their drunken, hopped-up jalopies up and down Main Street, leaving delinquent tyre tracks across respectable driveways, and causing young girls to forget their upbringing.

Naturally, this nightmare of society over-run by crazed hot-rodders made very good box office. Vicarious interest ran high in the twilight hoodlum world of loud cars and loose girls, and films with titles like *Hot Rod Girl*, *Dragstrip Girl* and *Hot Rods to Hell* were rushed into production.

Hot Rod Rumble in 1957 was a classic of its kind.

Chevrolet evolution. *Above:*
The 1956 Chevy Bel Air.
Below: The 1957 Chevy Bel
Air.

Above: A 1958 Chevy Biscayne. *Below:* A 1959 Chevy Impala. Setting the size for large American cars for years to come, the Impala's dimensions represented a challenge to other auto designers. However, at speeds of 90 mph the back had a tendency to lift off the ground.

Above: A 1959 Chevrolet Biscayne with continental kit (an optional extra). *Below:* A 1958 Chevrolet Impala with continental kit. Note the Impala was the only car with *three* triple tail lights.

Above: Tail light detail on a
1956 Chevy.

A 1959 Chevrolet Impala.

This 1959 Chevrolet Impala is more than eighteen feet in length. *Above:* A door detail. *Below:* The rear, featuring the divided gull wing tail.

Above and below: A 1960 Chevrolet Biscayne. This model is differentiated from the Bel Air by its three, rather than two tail lights.

Fantasies of rocket-propelled motion. *Left:* A 1957 Dodge Custom Royal Lancer. *Above:* A 1958 Chevrolet Impala, customised with 1959 Cadillac tail lights. *Above right:* The 1963 Ford Galaxie 500. *Far right:* A 1964 Chrysler Turbine Experimental. This gas turbine car was treated as a serious project by Chrysler. The

design of the rear was
influenced by the intakes and
outlets of a jet engine, which
in turn inspired the 1964
Dodge Model Range. Fifty
models were built and loaned
to private drivers to assess
public opinion, but only nine
survive, the rest were
dismantled by Chrysler
engineers.

A 1960 Chevrolet Impala.

Styling details of fifties fronts. *Left:* A 1949 Cadillac Series 61 Club Coupe. *Right:* A 1956 Ford Fairlane.

Left: A 1956 Chevrolet Bel
Air. *Right:* A 1959 Ford
Fairlane 500.

Left: A Series 2 Hillman Super Minx 1966. *Right:* A 1960 mid-series Vauxhall Velox.

Left: A 1957 Chevy Bel Air.
Right: A 1959 Ford Galaxie.

Above: A 1959 Ford
Thunderbird. In 1958 Ford
restyled the Thunderbird from
the 1957 European-type
sports car to an all-American
four seater. Thunderbird sales
doubled, but this new heavier
styling gave the car an
unsporting extra weight.
Below: A 1958 Chevrolet Bel
Air with a custom paint job
and tail lights.

'The scene is a party somewhere in teenland,' wrote Richard Staehling in a survey of teenage B-movies of the 1950s. 'Big Arny is uncouth and dresses flashy. His chick tells him to clean up, and he tells her to forget it. She does just that, riding home with another club member. On the way, a car that looks suspiciously like Big Arny's drives them off the road. Did Arny do it? If not, who did? Only on the day of the "big race" is the mystery solved . . . complete with actual footage of the Pomona drag strip.' If that wasn't delinquent enough, how about *Hot Car Girl* in 1958: 'It's good girls gone bad again, as four teens steal cars, selling them back to a junkyard dealer to make money. When one of the girls kills a motorcycle cop during a chicken race, the trouble really begins.'

Something of a vintage year, 1958 also produced *Dragstrip Riot*, described by its makers as 'the story of teenage youths who live as fast as their hot-rods will carry them'. After a minimal piece of plotting to get things moving (involving, opportunely, a motorcycle gang) we find that 'courage is measured in drag races, the climax building to a free-for-all between the two rival gangs'. All this is liberally salted with 'rock'n'roll numbers and actual flat races at Santa Barbara, California'. The only things the makers seem to have overlooked are drugs, girls and violent crime. Perhaps it was felt that the popular addition of 'real race footage' would compensate.

It was probably all far from the truth. On December 12th, 1958, the *LA Times* reported that police had broken up an 'impromptu speed meet' the previous night involving over 100 hot cars on the paved bed of the Los Angeles river. Most of those fined for breaking a by-law against driving on the dry riverbed were teenagers, accompanied by their wives and girlfriends. 'We can't race our cars on the streets,' said one, 'so we come here where we won't be in anyone's way. The drag strips are closed during the week. The police should supervise this deal and let us race here.' It would seem that the fellow was a model hot-rodder. 'We scarcely had time to warm up,' he complained morosely.

More in keeping with the fears of middle America was the riot that occurred in San Diego in 1960 when police used tear gas to disperse a mob of 3,000 that had gathered to watch some street races on an uptown thoroughfare. The crowd had congregated by word-of-mouth to protest at the closure of a local drag strip. Calls for city sponsorship of a strip as a result of the incident moved Mayor Charles Dail to retort: 'I've never felt it necessary to show kids how fast an automobile will go.'

Nor, by then, was there any need to. They had found out for themselves. The hot-rod had become an amorphous creation, no longer purely a hopped-up Ford roadster. Engines like the big-block Chevy, the Chrysler Hemi and the Cadillac and Oldsmobile V8s were being dropped into any available body and 'blown' by the addition of ram-chargers and outsize headers. It was no longer necessary to bore and measure and modify for speed; bolt-on equipment could be bought over the counter. It was not uncommon to wake from a hellish din the previous night and find the words 'start' and 'finish' painted on the road outside. By 1965, Los Angeles Police Department citations for 'speed contests' were running at a rate of over 2,000 a year – this can only have been a small percentage of the actual number of infractions.

The hot-rod mecca of the time was Bob's drive-in on Van Nuys Boulevard. On a Friday night, cars would queue along several blocks for an empty slot, surrounded by the inevitable crowds of onlookers. Inside, the lore, the legends, and the times and places of street races, would be told by jaws chomping on Big Boy hamburgers.

Writing in the *LA Times* in 1966, reporter Rob Ross recorded a typical pre-race ritual:

'Think you can take my Ford?'

'Think so,' Stretch replies.

'So do I,' says Pops, 'but I'll race you anyway – if you give me two car lengths.'

'I ain't gonna give you nothing,' Stretch says.

'My transmission is shot, the clutch is all torn up, and you come here with your ram-charger asking *me* for space.'

'I ain't got no ram-charger,' Pops protests.

'Show me,' Stretch challenges.

'No, man,' says Pops.

Eventually, after much haggling, a deal is struck. No space, but Stretch's girlfriend, who is really an experienced street racer, will drive his car. The race is set for 3.00 a.m. at Century and El Segundo. The bet is $300.

To Stretch, thirty-two-year-old owner of a modified '62 Corvette and president of the informal Western Avenue Street Racing Association, the street race was a way of life. To the numerous drive-in hot-rod teenagers of the era, it was simply the prevailing method of youthful outburst. Rob Ross quotes a policeman watching the traffic at Bob's: 'There's just not much we can do about it. If two cars pull even at a light, and somebody challenges somebody . . . The problem is that these kids have never seen death. They don't know that their lives can be snuffed out just

Above: A 1955 Packard
Clipper. *Below:* A 1959
Cadillac Sedan DeVille.

Above: A 1957 Chevrolet Bel Air Convertible. *Below:* A 1959 DeSoto Diplomat Deluxe (export only).

like *that*.'

Wally Parks had shown them speed, and more speed, in the surprisingly safe (compared to Grand Prix or the street) confines of the drag strip. The first NHRA-organised drag races took place in 1948 on a disused strip of the Goleta airfield near Santa Barbara. A quarter-mile from the start there was a hump in the strip, and the winner was whoever hit the hump first. The following year, when the races moved, with official blessing, to the Orange County airfield, the quarter-mile became standard. Other distances were tried but the lengths of these old runaways determined the optimum racing distance. Later on, there would be other refinements to the contests: up to sixty classes of competition allowing almost anyone to join in, and the test of 'terminal speed', a top speed measured through 132 feet across the finish (66 ft each side) that allowed, at times, for both cars to win.

'In the early days we used rolling starts,' Wally Parks recalled. 'But it was rare for both cars to hit the starting line together. The next advancement was the standing start. It proved popular, but it also proved expensive to many car owners. The sudden acceleration created a rash of broken rear axles, drive shafts and transmissions.'

This precipitated the era of specialised drag racing vehicles. The more dedicated drivers began to rebuild their roadsters, coupés and saloons with larger, heavy-duty rear axles, adding at the back fat treadless racing 'slicks' for extra traction. In due course this developed into the classic dragster configuration: a long, low lightweight front trailing back to the engine mounted right in front of the rear axle so as to do away with the drive shaft, and the driver sitting just ahead of the engine.

By this time, pro-fuel had become common and drag racing had come a long way from the streets. 'The "Bean Bandits", a group of about twenty Mexican boys from the San Diego area, began to experiment with fuel mixtures,' says Parks. 'They were winning everything in sight until the opposition learned their tricks. Those were the beginnings of fuel dragsters.'

Drag racing started as a healthy participatory event – loose speed meets at which winning was secondary to the smell and the noise and the thrashing of the cars. A traffic-light type of starting signal recalled its illegitimate origins. The divine burst of pure acceleration as the pedal hit the metal was its only logic. A race every few minutes (or less) kept the action at a pitch, and as the quarter-mile times shrank to a handful of neck-twisting seconds in the 1970s, the

crowds grew to levels that rivalled those of baseball. Drag racing is now quite probably, as its boosters have long proclaimed, America's biggest spectator sport.

Chronologically parallel to the hot-rod, parked side by side in places like Bob's drive-in, was the custom car. In the decade and a half that began with Truman and ended with Kennedy, the car-crazy youth of America applied time, money and maverick ingenuity to the creation of a wild public display of screaming metal. The motor car had become the dominant focus of American life; to take it and mould it into something unique was to stake a claim to the throbbing possibilities of that life, to snatch an individual identity from the huge machine press of comformity.

The custom car had hitherto been the exclusive mark of the well-heeled. The kings and princes of Europe and the rajahs of India had their Rolls-Royce, Hispano-Suiza and Mercedes-Benz limousines tailored in exquisite detail. The new nobility of America, the Hollywood movie stars, with no tradition of aristocratic reserve, no lineage of carriage and landau to draw on, could indulge in more dashing, more flamboyant, more flagrantly eye-catching exhibitions of their taste and standing. There were also more of them, and thus more individuality to be served, which allowed for the coach-building tradition to prosper in California when it died away elsewhere.

The movie colony's need to create striking images in the public and local eye supplied work for firms like the Earl Carriage Works (from which Harley Earl would later graduate to Detroit) and the Walter Murphy coachworks. Murphy's style was smooth and restrained. His windscreens had a few degrees more rake than everybody else's, and the tops of his roadsters folded down under discreet covers that created an uninterrupted curve from the back of the two-seat passenger compartment to the rear bumper. The rear wheels disappeared under wing panels, emphasising the clean, low sweep of the body. A Murphy-bodied Packard, Lincoln or Duesenberg was *the* car to own in pre-war Hollywood.

Status, or the desire to emulate the trappings of status, cannot alone explain how the custom car progressed from being the toy of the wealthy élite to the hobby of what seemed at times like the whole post-war west coast generation. Yet the smooth, uncluttered, low-slung roadsters of Walter Murphy, Dutch Darrin and the Coachcraft company were undoubtedly the stylistic starting point for the first teenage customs. These older, established coachbuilders were usually commissioned to create something like a European sports car for their clients, and their work was expensive. But after the war, adapting the golden proportions with a freer hand, a new kind of bodyshop came into being, sometimes staffed by a few old craftsmen, but more often by young, eager, apprentice bodybenders. With no fancy storefronts to maintain, they were in tune with the wishes and the means of a different sort of customer. The winged victory grille of the '49 Ford was all right for the man who had dutifully bought his war bonds, but active service merited a more glamorous and heroic contour.

This was most easily achieved by the rake of speed. When the shape of the motor car went from lean and tall to fat and round in the late 1930s, it was found that lowering the body gave a sleeker look. So began the business of cutting down the roof pillars (chopping), lowering the body on the chassis by cutting it away and rewelding (channelling), and removing a horizontal section from all the way around the middle of the body (sectioning). The voluptuous curves and bulging wings, plus the availability and good repair, of late 1930s and 1940s' Fords, Mercurys and Chevrolets made these cars the ideal subjects. In the late 1940s,

people like Link Paola, Jimmy Summers and Harry Westergard took the fad, that had begun with the hot-rod and spread to regular cars, of stripping off the chrome and smoothing down the line a step farther by judicious application of the welding torch.

Come the 1950s, this essential tool cut an ever more radical and alarming path through acres of carefully ordained, annually updated Detroit sheet metal. Who were the customers of this burgeoning backyard enterprise? Initially, perhaps, a few automobile fanatics who hung out with the crowd that screeched in and out of drive-ins and ran support at the drag strips. With maybe only a ten-year-old sedanette to work on instead of a genuine hot-rod, they could nevertheless share in the action by doing to the sedanette what their peers were doing to their own souped-up highboys. Pretty soon, you were either a 'restylist', or you were nowhere.

The possession of, or access to, a car by almost all middle-class teenagers of sixteen or over would have been an unimaginable gluttony in the confined and relatively close-knit towns and cities of Europe, but in the new sprawling post-war suburban dormitories of America, it was the vital means of youthful congrega-

A 1959 Ford Fairlane.

While American cars of the late fifties seemed to place no limits on design extravagance, British manufacturers pursued more sober design policies, occasionally allowing for the use of US styling details in miniature. *Above:* The Mark II Zephyr 1959/62. *Below:* A 1964 Jaguar. The well-heeled car-maker successfully resisted the encroachments of vulgar Americanisms.

tion. Inevitably, the car became part of the fun; sometimes the only fun. The whole structure of teenage society, and much of its competitive excitement (in more ways than one) was based on the all-important, all-pervasive automobile.

Novelist Nancy Friday remembers the mating dance of her youth conducted, not at the local hop, but on the local roads, where cars full of boys would cruise and chase and flirt with cars full of girls. 'The cars brought us together,' she recalled, 'but also kept us separate and intact.' Venturing alone into a car with a boy was an anxious thrill: 'There was an awful lot of weighty decision-making in those cars ... Even now when I get in a car with another man – not the man to whom I'm married – I still feel a certain zing inside at the thunk of the door.' Chuck Berry expertly trapped the frustrations of this automotive seduction game in songs like *Maybellene* and *You Can't Catch Me*; sly, knowing allegories of cars and girls.

With all the terrible weight of adolescent male sexuality riding in them, it's hardly surprising that these cars came to be such a peacock display of machismo, daring and style. A little imagination, and the discarded mass-production car became a Daytona record-breaker, a squat, mean, muscular coupé or a fur-lined, curb-hugging girl-trap. Restyling ran from 'mild' to 'wild': stripping the trim, welding the seams, moulding or tunnelling the lights deep in the body, swapping the grille for a chrome tube job from Western Auto, adding moon discs or Oldsmobile Fiesta hubcaps to the front wheels and covering the rear ones with wing panels, chopping, channelling or sectioning, and covering the result in lustrous, sexy paint highlighted by pinstripes, scallops and flames.

In some areas, and at different times, the aesthetic was minimalist, in other areas at other times it was add-on. Detroit shovelled on the chrome; the kids tore it off, and then, instead, chromed their engines. Detroit introduced panoramic windscreens; the kids cut theirs down to the size of postbox slots. Restyling was the automotive equivalent of the ducktail greased-back haircut, defying modesty, decorum and engineering logic. Often it was informed by a mad sense of humour; a pseudo-beatnik craziness later exemplified by the work of Ed Roth.

The inspiration for these customs came from many sources: from the drag strip and speed trial; from the GM Motorama dream cars; but mostly from car magazines like *Hot Rod, Hop-Up, Rod & Custom* and *Honk!*, many of them a handy 5″ × 8″ size which could slip neatly between the covers of a high-school textbook. These magazines regularly displayed the work of the Barris brothers, Joe Bailon, Gene Winfield, Joe Wilhelm, Dean Jeffries, Gil Alaya, Neil

Above left: British Ford Popular (customised). *Above right:* Rear detail of British Ford Capri Classic.

Strange customs. *Opposite above:* This BMW Isetta 300 'Bubble Car' of the late fifties, similar to many produced in Britain at the time, was a response to short-lived fears of the first oil shortage precipitated by the Suez Crisis. The relentless quest for customising novelty has seen this rare model transformed into a bizarre showpiece. *Opposite below:* A mid-sixties Chevrolet Corvette Sting Ray, sporting features borrowed from the drag strips: a pair of fat rear 'Slicks' and not one but two super-chargers. *Above:* Eschewing the zanier extremes, this classic 'blown' 1956 Chevrolet sports a single chromed super-charger.

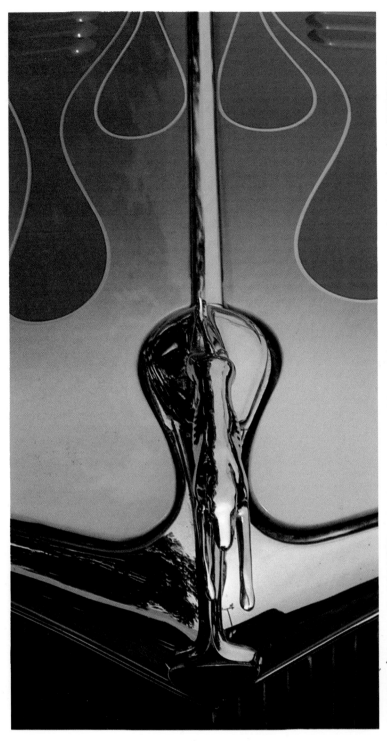

Custom paintwork began with
the introduction of trick paints
using simple motifs such as
flames and pin-striping.
Left: A hood (bonnet) detail of
a 1934 customised Ford.
Right: A customised 1939
Ford.

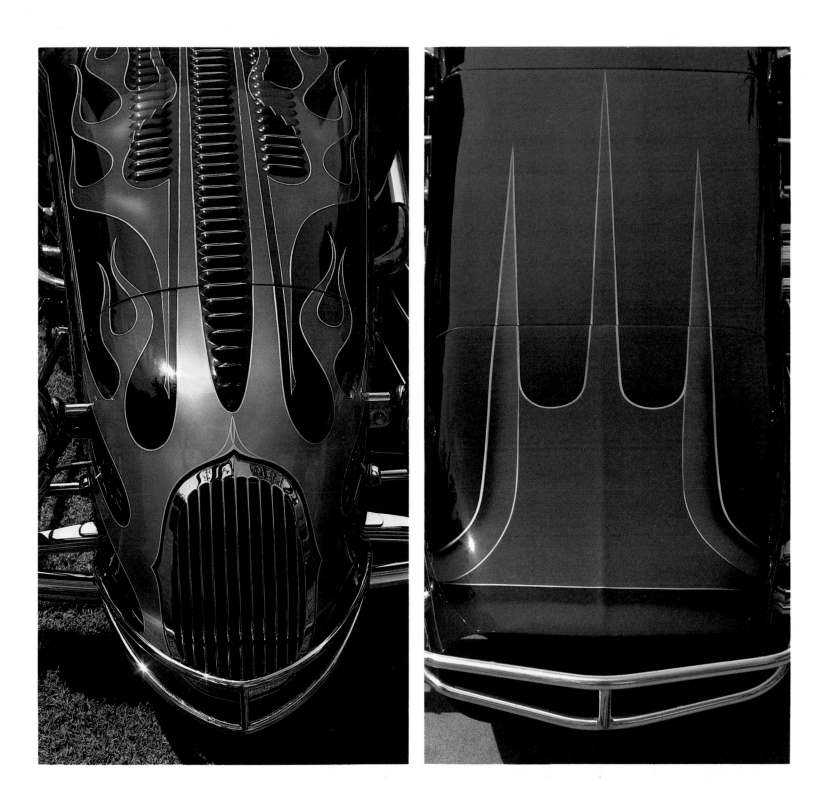

Above: Twenties Model T
Fords were the basis of these
heavily customised racers,
styled on the popular oval
track racing cars.

Emory and others from the west coast homeland of the boss custom.

In 1952, *Hop-Up* asked some of them which of Detroit's 1951 models they liked best, and what changes they would make for 1952. Invariably, the reply to the latter question was . . . *lower, longer.* 'I like the Chevy,' said Gil Alaya. 'In '52 I'd like to see about five inches taken out of the sides . . . lowered two inches; I'd also like cutaway doors, upsweep rear fenders and a narrower body.' The late Sam Barris wanted to take the Chevy even further: 'I'd like to see it about eight inches longer in back and about six inches in front. Seating down between the frame . . . everything push-button. Simple grille, and a lot less height between the ground and the top of the hood.' Neil Emory of Valley Custom thought the Ford Victoria the nicest car for the price: 'A good section job on one of those would really make it look great; say about four inches out of the side and, of course, lowered . . . simpler grille, less chrome . . . and lower.'

Valley Custom in Burbank, as may be surmised from Neil Emory's remarks, specialised in the most tortuous of all restyling techniques, the horizontal section. This meant cutting out a band of metal from right round the body and its supports and joining the top and bottom halves back together. Usually, this could not easily be done in a straight line, and it required careful measurements and consideration of all the clearances inside the body. Apart from some minor detailing and the usual chrome reduction, a good section job was often all that Valley Custom did to a car; but the results, which made their name in the early 1950s, were timeless. Refined American sports coupés were now comparable to the best work of their contemporaries in Italy's Ghia and Pininfarina studios.

Sam and George Barris opened their workshop in Lynwood after learning the craft from Harry Westergard in Sacramento. In 1949, Sam Barris lowered the top of his Mercury coupé and, when the car appeared soon afterwards on the cover of *Motor Trend*, it caused a sensation. The top chop became the Barris hallmark of the early 1950s. Countless chopped Fords and Mercurys from 1941 to 1948 rolled out, looking squashed and angry, on to the forecourt of Barris Kustoms.

George ('spell it with a K') Barris was a tireless booster of the custom car, but more especially of the Barris Kustom car. While Sam, who died in the mid 1960s, supervised the workshop, George Barris was in the front office, sketching out the details of a custom with a client, organising coverage for Barris cars in magazines and exposure at the car shows. He learned the publicity value of an extravagant custom in the mid 1950s when he built the 'Golden Sahara', originally a '52 Lincoln. With its glass-covered cockpit, gullwing doors and impossibly long rear wings (not to mention TV, telephone, tape recorder and bar), the car appeared as well suited to space travel as boulevard cruising. It resembled the earlier Ford FT-Axmos dream car but was sadly unable to take advantage of Ford's envisioned compact nuclear power source.

The Golden Sahara also wore a unique pearlescent paint job. Barris had seen the pearl paint – made originally with fish scales and available only from Japan – used on a billboard. It was applied to the car over a white undercoat, sealed with clear lacquer, and then left out to dry. In the hot sunshine, the fish scales turned yellow; so Barris gold-plated the trim, and called it the Golden Sahara. The car was an unusually radical custom for Barris at the time, though later there would be many such wild essays in unconventional and exaggerated styling.

More typical Barris Kustoms of the mid 1950s were the '40s Mercury coupés chopped and channelled and sprayed with candy-apple paint – the first trick paint of the 1950s, so named for its deep red colour achieved by spraying clear lacquer mixed with red toner over a metallic undercoat. Credit for its invention has been claimed by Joe Bailon, Barris and Emmet Glasgow, who worked at Barris Kustoms. Barris says he got the idea from Christmas tree ornaments; Bailon remembers seeing such a finish on the drums of the swing bands. He exhibited a candy job on a '41 Chevy at the Oakland Roadster Show of 1952, and soon both he and Barris were marketing this ubiquitous paint in a rainbow of colours and handy spray cans.

No other customiser of the decade could hope to compete with Barris' gaudy entrepreneurial style. In 1955, he bought the wreck of James Dean's Porsche for $2,500, planning to re-sell each part. Barris had met Dean when he customised a hot-rod for the film *Rebel Without a Cause*, and by the early 1960s, he and his cars, and most of his clients, were exclusively show business. He had always liked to cut a loud profile, and now he had the opportunity. His cars were either custom-built to be towed on trailers to the custom car shows, or custom modifications for a showbiz clientèle – of which he kept a gallery of photos of car, star and Barris. If someone wanted a spectacular or zany auto for a car show or an advertising campaign or for film or TV – such as the Batmobile, based on the Lincoln Futura dream car of 1955 – they came to Barris. His more famous cars were available as scale model plastic kits, and he

OUTH FIREBALL 500

gained pop art respectability when Tom Wolfe wrote about him in *The Kandy-Kolored Tangerine-Flake Streamline Baby*, the title of which refers to a semi-custom 1960 Chevrolet painted with Tangerine Flake, one of Barris' patent Kandy Kolors.

Detroit had discovered the custom car and the hot-rod – or as they saw it, the youth market – not long before

Tom Wolfe. At first, they scratched their heads, sensing its potential size, but unable to grasp its desires. It was evidently there to be exploited because some people were already doing so. The 1960s would see the decline of the personal, driveable, home-built, self-styled fun custom and the arrival of the professional and factory special.

The custom cult had by then covered the country, with the help of magazines and car shows featuring the

George Barris, self-styled King of the Kustomisers, in 1966, sitting in his Fireball 500.

The painstaking perfection of baroque custom paintwork. Murals, pin-stripes, scrolls, red and yellow flames – the traditional elements of custom paintwork – have evolved into an abstract fairground style, the cars themselves have become kinetic day-glo showpieces. Once embarked on a custom paint job, the true customiser is rarely satisfied

with just a coat of Candy-Apple or Metal-Flake: nobody ever told them that less is more. The ornate decoration of these early British and American Fords and the cooler treatment of the seventies muscle cars is typical of the fanciful improvisation on a theme and the fanatical attention to detail.

The true customiser is not content until every available inch of the car has been personalised. *Above left:* A 1937 Chevy boasts a carved leather dashboard, ivory gear stick and six extra engine gauges. *Above right:* The fur-lined custom cocoon, including a chain-link steering wheel, billiard ball gear stick and the inevitable furry dice – hung, just for a change, from the dashboard.

work of Daryl Starbird, Dave Stuckey and Bill Cushenberry in Kansas, and Dave Puhl and the Alexander brothers in Illinois. The first official car show took place at the Armory in LA's Exposition Park in 1948, sponsored by the SCTA and a Hollywood publicity agency, one of whose partners was Robert Petersen, who was about to publish the first issue of *Hot Rod* magazine. The following year, a 'hot-rod exposition' was held in Northern California; it went on to become the long-running Oakland Roadster Show. Shows such as these and the many that followed, initially loose, enthusiastic affairs, first popularised and then commercialised the custom car.

Gradually, a show circuit came into being, spreading across the country and promoted, sometimes directly, by the magazines, whose appetite for new customs was large. Customisers soon saw the benefits to business of winning what was at first just a slap on the back from fellow restylists and started building special or radical customs to show off their abilities.

The quest for show points reached ludicrous heights. Cars were set on clouds of cottonwool, bathed in sympathetic light, and finished in such extravagant detail that they had to be towed to the venues. Promoters started paying tow-money for a spectacular custom that was bound to draw the crowds; before long they were sponsoring show cars themselves and even paying top customisers for personal appearances. Although the respected Oakland Roadster Show required that cars be capable of being driven on the road, others were not so purist. Dismayed by such professional competition, the teenage customiser began to lose interest in his own car. Customs, like hot-rods, went from being a participatory activity to a big-time spectacle.

At the same time, the endless and ever greater hoopla of the car shows created an accelerated cycle of custom fads. It was no longer enough to strip off the chrome, smooth down the body, and give the car a dazzling coat of paint. First, a few parts of the engine were chromed, to look like new racing goodies, then the whole engine was chromed, and then all the other bare metal was chromed, even, in the death, the entire underbody of the car!

After chrome, what? Upholstery. Everything that wasn't chromed was upholstered, even the wheel wells. The excesses of the legitimate motor industry of the late 1950s adversely affected the illegitimate industry, which was always ready to take things that much farther.

Paintwork, likewise, suffered from the shlock of the new, as craze after craze swept the shows and hence

the country. The reclusive Von Dutch, the first automobile muralist, used pinstriping initially to accent the custom line; but over the years his fine brushwork lines grew more ornate, and turned into curling, liquid scrolls or scallops. Highlighted by contrasting colours, these designs became kinetic flames that spread from under the bonnet and behind the wheels to envelop the entire body of the car, which, in turn, became an abstract, swirling wash of colour. The custom car swam in a sea of blazing, unnatural shades of violet, purple, red and yellow. There was no longer any need to own a restyled car, for a custom paint job on a production car was sufficient to make heads turn.

Variety was now a commonplace; individuality was available over the counter in cans, decals and add-on fibreglass mouldings. The use of fibreglass allowed customisers to sell cheap, identical custom kits for a popular model of car, and even entire custom bodies. Ed Roth was the first in this field. He built his customs like a sculptor. Working in clay on a wooden buck, he would then take a mould of the finished body which could be repeated as many times as there were buyers. Inspired by Roth's free-form 'weirdo' cars, Bruce Meyers designed a fibreglass body for a VW Beetle chassis in the early 1960s and called it the Dune Buggy. Customisers ruefully admit it was the most popular custom of all time.

Some of the top customisers began to find their individual clients dwindling and Detroit walking through the door with contracts to build show cars to lure youngsters – pre-teens who bought the Revell kits of the outlandish customs of Barris, Roth and Starbird – to things like the Ford Custom Caravans of 1963 to 1965. The show cars by then were presenting such a static and unobtainable ideal, almost a caricature of the original, that interest shifted towards the drag strip. There, at least, the cars *did* something – they were toys that worked – and what they did could be copied by anyone with enough reckless teenage nerve, which flowed at the least stimulus. The car magazines of the early 1960s had sensed this change, and began to feature drag strip results in place of lists of car show winners.

The street custom, therefore, returned to its original inspiration of speed. The mechanics of a car rather than its clothing became the focus of customising attention; although, as had happened before, the cosmetic suggestion of speed was often enough: bulging hood scoops, airfoils and spoilers, fat tyres and other performance styling 'cues' borrowed from the drags. The war babies were about to mature into affluent, car-loving customers – by the summer of

Above: Detail on a British Ford Capri. *Below:* A pair of 'Frenched' aerials.

Sublime paint finish on a
1934 Ford.

Until the Chevy Corvette arrived in 1953, America had no modern production sports cars. The Corvette, with its lean continental lines and a nimble V8 engine in a fibre-glass body, was an immediate success. Ford soon followed Chevrolet's lead with the Thunderbird in 1955, but while the Corvette remained distinctly a sports car, the Thunderbird rapidly evolved the bulky lines of typical American cars of the time. *Above:* A 1958/1959 Ford Thunderbird. *Below:* A 1962 Chevy Corvette. With its fibre-glass body and a new 327-ci V8 engine, this model was a formidable sportster, to start with, but it has been fitted with a super-charger just to make sure.

Above: The four ages of go-faster custom styling details: louvres, flames, hood-scoops and rectangular headlamps.
Below: A customised 1958 Corvette modelled on the XP-700 Corvette dream car designed by Bill Mitchell and exhibited that year.

Custom styling details. *Above left:* A British Vauxhall, the original PA Cresta. *Below left:* A set of side pipes and a restrained custom paint job. *Above:* Two examples of mural work on late model 'Muscle Cars'.

Above and opposite: Details on a 1962 Chevrolet Corvette.

1968 half of the US population was under thirty – and drag racing had lost its delinquent taint and become a recognised sport. This was all that was needed to persuade the motor industry to make its bow in the newly defined youth market with the Pontiac GTO, the first of America's muscle cars.

No sub-cultural fad or live-wire teenage style could hope to compete with Detroit marketing money. The GTO, introduced in 1964, was simply a performance 'treatment' given to a standard Pontiac Tempest. For $300 extra you could buy the GTO package: floor-change, 389-ci engine, stiffer shocks, dual exhaust, bigger tyres and hood scoops. Another $75 bought better brakes and transmission. Introduced by John De Lorean after an idea from Jim Wangers, it was the first youth-oriented factory custom. Wangers, a former drag racer of the unofficial Pontiac team, also came up with a suitable launch gimmick. Before the car came out, he did a deal with a New York record company to release a record called *Little GTO*. Wangers wrote the lyrics himself, cramming them full of drag slang, and it was sung by Ronny and the Daytonas.

With some discreet financial inducement, *Little GTO* sold over a million copies, while the big GTO went on to sell 38,000 in its first year – the best-selling new model in Pontiac's history. This was not lost on the other manufacturers, who were soon embroiled in

a frantic, industry-wide horsepower race, the prize for which was the all-important first-time buyer. Despite an agreement by the manufacturers in 1955 forbidding the support of auto racing, they had long since continued unofficially to sponsor independent teams in all fields. The attention of the first-time buyer, and his ensuing brand loyalty, was worth an estimated annual $25 million of unofficial sponsorship by Ford alone in the early 1960s. The success of the GTO proved to manufacturers that they should be chasing the youthful customer with performance figures, or at any rate performance styling, on the streets as well.

Moreover, the 'youthful' customer was not only the moneyed teenager. With all the clamour that surrounded the young generation of the late 1960s, youth lifestyles came to set the pace. Youth was synonymous with freedom and promiscuity in the minds of a good many middle-aged Americans; pleasures that had passed them by in the dark days before the Pill. In a society where you are what you drive, what better (or what other) way to express the mute, jealous desire to partake of this newfound social and sexual liberation than to drive a 'youthful' car? 'Don't think for a moment that we won't sell you a Camaro if you're over thirty,' ran a typically facile piece of ad copy. 'After all, it's not how young you are, it's how old you feel.'

Contemporary customs. *Above:* The recent trend towards customised vans offers acres of metal for painting and decoration. *Below:* The latest race-track styles quickly find their way onto street customs. *Opposite:* Traditional customising elements have become stylised in the extreme on this seventies Corvette; pin-striping no longer serves to emphasise the car's lines but has become ornate scroll-work; what were once representational flames have become an abstract decoration; the hood scoop just keeps growing. The four rectangular headlights are the latest custom fad, while the front spoiler and bulging wheel arches pay homage to the latest sports styles.

From fins to fastbacks to air-foils. *Above left:* The graceful curve of a 1963 Corvette Sting Ray. *Below left:* Air-foil on a modern Chevy Camaro. *Above right:* Air-foil on a late model Trans Am. *Far right:* Add-on moulded air-foil on a British Ford Capri.

Detroit muscle from the sixties. *Above and below:* One of the original muscle cars, this Shelby Mustang GT350, complete with a pair of Holley carbs under a detachable perspex hood (bonnet) scoop, was made in 1968. The first Shelby Cobras, basically performance modified versions of the 1965 Ford Mustang, were capable of speeds of up to 150 mph. *Opposite:* A supercharged 1968 Ford Mustang.

The Pontiac GTO, and its many imitators and successors, was bought at first by teenagers, and then, in much larger numbers, by older men who wanted to pass for teenagers. By 1968, the list of these muscle cars – huge, roaring beasts of rampant horsepower – was longer than the option list of a Cadillac: Ford's Fairlane Cobra, Torino GT, Mustang Mach I, Boss 302 and Boss 429; Chevrolet's Chevy II Nova SS, Camaro SS and Camaro Z/28; Dodge's Charger R/T and 500, Super Bee, Dart GTS, and Swinger; Buick's GS 350 and 400; Pontiac's Firebird HO and Trans-Am; Mercury's Cyclone CJ, Spoiler, Cougar XR-7 and Eliminator; Plymouth's Barracuda; Oldsmobile's 4-4-2 … and so it goes on. The names were a mixture of Grand Prix and US Supernational style numerical designation, the jargon of drag trappings, and pure, wicked fantasy. The relative merits of the cars, built for brute acceleration, cannot be sensibly debated. They were gross, bulging, aggressive slabs of brute mechanical power, and the most splendid and unbelievable of them all was the Plymouth Superbird, which came ex-works with a two-foot-high rear airfoil.

A cluster of stickers in one corner of the car indicated exactly which hot, esoteric performance extras the serious owner had under the bonnet. Street racing inevitably proliferated, although the more determined racers had graduated to interstate highways because of the speeds now involved. Manufacturers had to tread the line between a 'hot' name and the condemnation of city fathers, always stressing safety alongside performance, and distancing these particular cars from the rest of the company's products (but not *too* far) by creating special divisions and dealerships. However, they were not above allowing a member of the factory staff to take a specially set-up car out on the streets to covertly build its grass-roots reputation.

Exhaust emission regulations introduced in the late 1960s to protect the environment, and growing consumer campaigns for safety, inspired by Ralph Nader's 1966 book *Unsafe at any Speed*, would soon put an end to cars built solely for acceleration in a straight line. Insurance company pressures to lower horsepower – by then into the 500s and rising on some cars – slowed down the runaway muscle car. The Arab oil embargo of 1973, resulting not least in a nationwide 55 mph speed limit that is still in force, stamped out all but a few sad and limping cases.

Stranded by the gas crisis, harnessed by safety regulations, choked by environmental controls and impoverished by inflation, the American car is now a pitiful tin husk, emasculated and tamed by its Japanese and European cousins. The muscle car was to be the last and the greatest of all of Detroit's automotive fairground rides.

Above left: An early seventies Corvette: the hood (bonnet) bulge is factory standard.
Above right: One of the growth industries in customising in the seventies has been the fibre-glass kit car There's no telling what humble motor car lies beneath this futuristic body.

A late seventies Trans Am.
The power bulge on the hood
(bonnet) and the phoenix
mural are factory standard.

127

'What is good for the country is good for General Motors, and what is good for General Motors is good for the country.' – Charles Erwin Wilson before a Senate Armed Services Committee in 1952.

'Dear Bob,
We have a big gas-guzzling Lincoln Continental, a big gas-guzzling Ford LTD wagon, and a gas-guzzling Pontiac Catalina. I love to pull alongside a socialist 35-mpg and leave my engine running for venting my frustration at what is happening.' – Letter to Bob White's *Duck Book*, the gazette of US small-town patriotism.

American car production, the wellspring of the car culture and the litmus of Western industry, has fallen to its lowest level since the end of the Second World War. Glory has been sacrificed to utility, and styling has become subordinate to miles-per-gallon. Images in advertising of ocean liners and aeroplanes, beautiful women, effortless motion and bounteous technology, have been replaced as far as they ever can be by the praises of frugality and appeals to horse sense.

Back in the 1920s, Walter Engard, an Ohio car dealer, spelled out exactly what is at stake. 'Higher standards of living are built up through millions of individual extravagances,' he told the readers of *Motor* magazine. 'To keep America growing we must keep Americans working, and to keep Americans working we must keep them wanting; wanting more than the bare necessities; wanting the luxuries and frills that make life so much more worthwhile, and instalment selling (of automobiles) makes it easier to keep Americans wanting.'

You might think that the New Depression has tolled the final refutation of these great principles. But a glance at the latest models reveals that style, though it has undergone some abrupt and unexpected convulsions, still keeps people (not just Americans) wanting. The New Depression has merely hacked at a Hydra-headed automania. Even the Great Depression of the 1930s had, it turned out, scarcely more effect. Returning to Middletown in the mid 1930s, Robert and Helen Lynd found that the motor car had survived the crash virtually undented.

The Lynds were immediately struck by the fact that 'filling stations have become in ten years the most prominent physical landmarks'. Children no longer played in the streets and the prevailing sentiment, heard time and again, was that people would give up everything in the world but their car: 'If the automobile is by now a habit with the business class, a comfortable, convenient, pleasant addition to the paraphernalia of living, it represents far more to the working class; for the latter it gives the status which his job increasingly denies and, more than any other possession or facility to which he has assess, it symbolises living, having a good time, the thing that keeps you working.'

It is still true, particularly in Britain (though perhaps only because the stratification of British society is more apparent), that the most rabid manifestations of devotion to automania occur amongst the lower middle and working classes, especially the lower middle and working class youth. It is no less true that the car – despite the challenge of TV – is still the key to a great many recreational possibilities for all classes, but especially the young, who remain more interested in themselves and each other than in TV. Abandoning the car as a utility vehicle would obviously be impossible at present, and abandoning it as a source of entertainment and an expression of style would require a feat of superhuman self-denial that no one in their right mind would dare demand of the peoples of the industrialised West.

In the years preceding and following the Second World War, America – its landscape, its mores, its way of life – changed with a suddenness and finality that equalled the change wrought by the coming of the railways in the previous century. In 1930, Charles Merz wrote of a roving spirit that throbbed in the nation's veins: 'If we cannot rove for the purposes of settling a continent, we shall at least rove, daily and nightly, for the pleasure of seeing something, anything, or seeing nothing, and merely having been.'

To cater to this tendency and its newly accelerated means, there arose the infinitely recurring topography of turnpike, billboard, drive-in, motel and suburb; a world of reassuring sameness or of nightmare repetition.

In San Bernadino in 1940, two brothers from New

A 1946/7 Buick, photographed in a junk yard in California. In 1947 the automotive industry was back in full swing and selling almost as many vehicles as in the pre-war period.

A typical American urban
landscape.

Inns, each of their rooms, like a Big Mac, exactly like the one before, now host an average of 200,000 travellers every night. The *Sunday Times* included Wilson in a list of the 100 key figures of the twentieth century – not bad for someone who reputedly orders his dessert first so he can eat it while his steak is cooking.

The first drive-in cinema had opened in 1933, not in California but in New Jersey. Perhaps in an effort to compete with the powerful new fables of the big screen, the church, too, opened its doors to the car. The needs of a motorised population were soon served by drive-in restaurants, banks, grocery shops, laundries – everything except toilets. The increasing push-button engineering ease of the car wrought by powerful engines and automatic transmissions and even remote-controlled garage doors, had already turned it into less of a machine than a piece of architecture, and after the war it became a kind of living-room on wheels. This was, indeed, a desirable thing. 'The '49 Ford,' said the brochures, 'is a living-room on wheels!'

The franchise operations of McDonalds and Holiday Inn, and others that followed, did much to obliterate the regional culture of America. They arrived just in time to capitalise on the expanding suburbs and to take advantage of the interstate highway system; a network of 'townless highways' proposed in the 1940s as a solution to clogged and dangerous roads that resulted from the ad hoc roadside ribbon-develop-

England opened a hamburger stand. Eight years later, business was good, but Richard and Maurice McDonald decided it could be improved by converting the operation to a self-service drive-in. With the help of Ray Kroc, a former salesman for a firm that made a milkshake mixer that could mix up to six shakes at a time, they introduced the ethos of the Detroit production line to the hamburger. It was, in effect, nothing less than the Fordisation of food.

The word 'motel' (a corruption of motor-hotel) first came into use in the mid 1920s. It described the plasterboard roadside night-stops known in their early days as 'tourist cabins' – at first just an office and a row of tents, later an office and a row of cabins and several big signs – that gave rest to America's roving peoples. The Fordisation of the motel did not occur until 1951, when a Memphis real-estate developer named Charles Kemmons Wilson decided to build a motel with all the creature comforts he and his family had been unable to count on in the unpredictable motel stops of their recent vacation: TVs, telephones, cots for the kids, and swimming pools. He hired an architect, named his motel the Holiday Inn (after a Bing Crosby movie called *Holiday Inn* which he had seen the night before) and within two years he had built three more from the original plans. 'You just had to go by a Holiday Inn to get into Memphis,' he clucked. The 1,400 Holiday

Above: Three-dimensional advert for Uniroyal Tyres in Detroit. *Below:* Derelict gas station in California.

Above: A burn-up down the King's Road, London.

ment of towns and cities. Construction began in 1956 on the 41,000 miles of motorway and interchange linking every major US city. There was already, repetition, in the words of Lewis Mumford, 'a scorching ugliness of badly planned and laid out roads peppered with impudent billboards . . . a vast spreading metropolitan slum of multiple gas stations and hot dog stands; and on the highways, a conflict between speed, safety and pleasure.' The interstate system was supposed to cure all this, but was thwarted by the immutable law of cars and roads: the more cars you have, the more roads you build, but the more roads you build, the more cars you have.

Nor was America alone in this problem. Europe had fewer cars, but it also had less space. In Europe, as in America, mass-produced housing mushroomed on the edges of cities and towns, and the roads that were the arteries of the new suburbs quickly became choked by the car and littered with the roadside distractions of modern life. An urban sprawl came into being which historian A.J.P. Taylor characterised as being composed of 'little more than individual cars come to rest'. Most European cities and towns, and older American ones such as Boston and New York, were fortunate in having existing urban railway or bus systems that forestalled the crisis. But as economies, and thus car ownership, boomed in the 1950s, the

floridly symmetrical boulevards of Paris, Rome and Barcelona, the old, haphazard roads of London and Amsterdam, and the ancient cobbled mazes of many a European town experienced a recurring and ever-worsening thrombosis.

The middle classes have been able to escape this poisonous congestion by moving yet farther away from the old merchant centres of the cities and commuting to work in an air-conditioned cocoon. The poor, meanwhile, have become trapped in the disintegrating inner city. The car has effectively drained the vigour from those cities that were civilisation's greatest monuments and replaced them with a new monument to itself: the concrete and asphalt over-passes, under-passes, by-passes, gyratory systems, clover-leafs and six-lane motorways woven across the planet like the canals of Mars. One wonders what future archaeologists will make of a city like Los Angeles – once described as merely seventy-two suburbs in search of a city – whose population is now outnumbered by its cars.

The enforced economies of the early 1970s brought about a final disenchantment with (and since then, something of a wake for) the over-powered, over-sized, over-priced baroque automobile. It's still poss-

ible – for the very few – to buy a car powered by a race-bred V12 engine with carburettors like saxophones and the high-speed whine of insects at dusk, its body a mere ripple in the wind, its gears like a knife through butter. But the 1970 Cadillac Eldorado 8.2 with a 8,200-cc engine, the largest production car engine in the world . . . that now languishes in a cul de sac of engineering evolution. Something of a watershed was reached in 1976 with the Cadillac Eldorado, the last American convertible – a victim of the noise and pollution of congested traffic. Even the mighty Cadillac has now shrunken to a size scarcely bigger than the average European saloon.

Yet this has had no visibly diminishing effect on the endeavours of people, mostly young people, to style themselves through the medium of their cars, their cars being, apart from their clothes, the *only* medium available, and for Americans, who virtually live in them, the most visible. The mating rituals described by Nancy Friday and given vivid expression by Chuck Berry were not about to be foresaken merely because the dimensions of the car and its possibilities for personal enhancement and individual glorification had changed.

To this day, certain preordained stretches of America's roads come alive on certain nights to the squeal of tyres, the gunning of motors, the slamming of doors, the shouts and giggles of teenage life. Nowadays, though, the only supercharged things about most of the cars are the stereos. Nevertheless tradition endures, kept alive by the 'Low Riders' of East LA's Spanish-American population.

Following the great example of their forebears, but forced to circumvent stricter vehicle regulations, they have the suspension systems of their cars rigged with powerful hydraulic jacks to lower the body at the flick of a switch like a channelled 1950s custom. Not all of them can afford the substantial mechanics involved so the alternative, also practised in the 1950s, is a torch job. You turn up at the garage having collected all the members of your gang and, with everybody in the car, a blowtorch is applied to the suspension springs until the desired minimal ground clearance is reached for cruising Whittier Boulevard.

The cars of East LA are big family sedans, late model cars covered in new paint and extra lacquer and trimmed with glistening chrome sidepipes. According to state law, the chassis of a car must be above the lower edge of the wheel rim, but the hydraulics employed by gangs allow it to be lowered to within a centimetre of the ground. Another illegal activity is scraping. This is done by welding a piece of metal onto the back axle. The car is then lowered using the hydraulics and dragged along the boulevard. These

Friday night on Van Nuys Boulevard, Los Angeles.

'bad rides' leave a trail of dangerous sparks (right next to the fuel tank) as they nightly cruise the boulevards, bucking up and down like stallions on their juiced suspensions to the apparent delight of any nearby girls. Black and Hispanic Americans, for whom the car is often a way of attaining the status denied them elsewhere, tend to favour large and expensive sedans, decorated and embroidered with the trappings of a lurid, fake opulence; a sad appropriation of the gauche colours and ersatz materials found in upper-middle class American homes. Not for nothing are the Cadillac bordellos of the superfly gangster a movie cliché.

Deprived of speed as a means of asserting their fragile, bursting egos by mandatory emission control equipment that lowers a car's performance, the American teenager has been forced to turn elsewhere. Few of them can afford the tax-weighted prices of fast European cars, and hopping up an emission-controlled engine is difficult and costly (though it can and is done). The end of the horsepower race has left the road open for the rebirth of customising; attention turned from engines to bodywork.

With speed now a taboo, the look of speed is not quite so eagerly cultivated as it was in the past. The Trans-Am road racer look of a low, sleek body bedecked with airfoils and spoilers, and resting on wide tyres covered by flared and sculpted fenders, is the evolution of an evergreen racing inspiration and is now supplied in fibreglass kit form for most of the popular models of cars – even, in some cases, supplied in place on the car by the manufacturers themselves. A newer inspiration has been the rugged and ready look of the off-road four-wheel-drive car, achieved in no time at all with an old pick-up truck and fitting in well with the late 1970s stereotyped masculine ideal of the strapping cow-puncher and the trends towards fresh air sports and rude living out there in the rediscovered romance of Marlboro country. For all their supposed individuality, perhaps there is an innate conservatism in the custom breed.

Inevitably, the time came to paint the pick-up truck, and with all that sheet metal to adorn, the old urges surfaced once more. The extravagant detailing and wild fantasies that were typical of the early 1960s customs have come back in vogue, encouraged in part by a peripheral auto industry of individuality. Resurrecting and restyling a vehicle half-digested by the accelerated cycle of consumption – which was once a marginally subversive activity – has now been heavily commercialised.

From pick-up trucks – with all that space to apply the welding torch, the huge palette of spray paints and the imagination – to vans, an even larger canvas and an even bigger fad. The customised van – a bizarre

Cruising on Whittier Boulevard, Los Angeles. *Above:* An early fifties Styleline Chevy.

juxtaposition of the rustic and the ultra-modern (desert landscapes painted on the side of space pods) – is a personal and personalised mobile environment representing the ultimate destination of the four-wheeled lifestyle. No longer just the living-room, but the whole home on wheels: living-room, bedroom, kitchen and bathroom. Here are mobile caves decorated with a profuse and loving finery of vinyl, fur, chrome, perspex, lacquer, wood and metal. Nowadays, they can even be bought straight from the showroom. The custom van was initially a mid-western phenomenon, but it has caught on fast. On the east and west coasts, it now vies with the rather more up-market pastime of restoration. Once lavished solely on vintage models, the attentions of the restorer have moved on to the post-war classic, of which more and more are discovered as the years go by.

Interest in the preservation and usually careful driving of cars of the late 1940s through to the early 1960s was animated in 1973 by George Lucas' celluloid requiem for an innocent and romantic teenage world, *American Graffiti*. In Europe more so, but also in the US, *American Graffiti* ushered in a nostalgic revival of the shapes, sounds and styles of the 1950s. Except that in Europe it wasn't a revival so much as a postdated copying of something that at the time could only be envied from an impossible, impoverished distance. *American Graffiti* arrived in Europe like a time capsule to be plundered for the strange and wonderful ephemera of a vanished era, its treasures sorted, adapted and worn with the glee of a tribe discovering the remains of a dead but once mighty civilisation.

In Britain, Belgium, Holland and Sweden, the custom car existed before *American Graffiti*, but as an isolated, oddball obsession. In Europe in the 1950s there was little opportunity for a car-oriented youth lifestyle to thrive as it did in the US – Europe was neither geographically nor economically suited. Some of the extravagance of legitimate US car styling did, however, rub off. The Vauxhall and the Peugeot grew tame fins in imitation of their Yankee cousins, modest traces of rocket styling reflected the humble attempts of Europe to follow the superpowers into space with the launch of the Telstar satellite. And within the limits of European roads, the Ford of the late 1950s got as big as it decently could.

Europe was still too busy rebuilding itself to be building monuments to itself. In any case, the monuments to its civilisation were more likely to be stationary rather than mobile. But the national character of car building at the time did result in some idiosyncratic displays of national identity: the staid, classical lines of Jaguar or Wolseley in Britain; the modern curves of a

Above: A 1957 Chevy.

135

The following pictures were taken in a California junk yard. *Above:* The remains of a 1957 Metropolitan. *Below:* A 1954 Buick.

Above left: Wing detail on a 1960 Imperial. *Above right:* Rear light detail on a 1958 Chevy Biscayne. *Below:* A 1958 Pontiac Bonneville.

Above: Mercury 1946/8.

Citroën or Renault in France; the apologetic humility of the VW Beetle in Germany.

Any notion of good design, though, was synonymous with Italy. The studios of Pininfarina, Bertone and later Ghia and Ital were called in whenever a manufacturer wanted the badge of 'good design' – not only manufacturers in Italy and the rest of Europe but in America and Japan too. For their part, the Italian stylists were not so snobbish as to hold the American car in contempt for its vulgarity and ostentation. Like their counterparts in companies throughout Europe, they were basically enamoured of the emotive power of car styling, and couldn't help but envy the most emotive and unrestrained of all car styling, nor resist incorporating at least some of its features.

They shared this envy with those who saw American cars in movies and magazines, or glimpsed the real thing around embassies and military bases – doubly powerful symbols of wealth and freedom when cast against the drizzle and frugality of Britain. And hot-rod movies celebrated a noise and a style and an activity as young and liberating as rock'n'roll. It was bound to catch on.

By the mid 1960s, there were a few people like Geoff Jago building street rods with parts cannibalised from British cars and plans gleaned from measuring the pictures in American magazines. They congre-gated for the first British custom car show in 1966 – in an underground car park in Hyde Park. The most popular motor sport in Britain at the time was the motor rally – like the US stock car races, a test of a production car's metal. Popular in terms of being accessible to the amateur – unlike Grand Prix which drew more spectators – it spawned customising trends that ran to a profusion of headlights and mechanical refinements but not much further. Within a few years, though, the rally-style Mini had become the Carnaby Street Mini and there were even some rainsoaked but undaunted Beach Buggies to be met.

As the new decade began, Britain acquired a home-grown custom car magazine and its first official custom shows, along with a few more of the American techniques and even a US-style drag strip started with the help of some expatriate Americans. It took *American Graffiti*, though, to give the necessary sharp definition to something that could only previously be garnered from hazy recollections and static photographs. The film precipitated the cult of the 1950s' American car in Britain, and also the cult of American-style customising of British cars, especially those of the late 1950s and early 1960s that already possessed a crypto-American style. It showed people what the look was, and what you did when you had it.

Scattered enthusiasts of the American car were

Above: Kaiser 1947/8. *Below:*
Grille detail on a 1950 Buick:
'The Million Dollar Grin'.

Above and below: Front and
back of a 1951 Studebaker.

united for the first time by *American Graffiti* – often literally right outside the cinema. Initially it was enough to drive *any* American car, but US auto fanaticism now convenes mostly around the distinctive cars of the *Graffiti* era. There are fierce allegiances, small rivalries, freewheeling associations and plenty of actual clubs, their members bitten by the joy of real steel and haunted by the ideal of an automotive full-stop: the Supreme Transport.

This is a very elusive quality and, when it does finally solidify, the obsession can just as easily begin again. It could be an authentic gutsy little hot-rod, or an acknowledged classic maintained in showroom condition since 1963. It needn't be perfect, and certainly not discreet, but it would have to have *all* the extras. A Cadillac Eldorado Biarritz of 1959 might do. Or it could be a Chevy Monza Spyder with a mid-mounted 454-ci big-block engine, painted matt black with no chrome at all, so the owner could hit the motorway at night without lights, using a Vietnam infra-red visor for vision, and go past everything else like a silhouette at 140 miles per hour!

Owning an American car in Britain is no mere fanciful pastime. The first thing that strikes the unwary British motorist about an American car is its enormous size. The wild colours, the fins, the chrome come second. What really strikes deep down at the civilised European sensibility is the sheer, brute, menacing *bulk* of the thing. On European roads the American car seems cramped and constrained like a beast in a cage. Sensible road users panic when they see one coming the opposite way down a narrow street. Like some American tourists in their garish check pants, these cars provoke feelings of mute impoverished resentment. In the mind of the sensible road user – whose car is attached to a rigid hierarchy of taste and status – there is often something profoundly disturbing about an American car. If one *needed* a big car, one would buy something sensible like a Volvo. But some American cars confound these values. Their owners have declared a car war on the proper instincts of society, proclaimed themselves outside the reach of the advertising copywriters.

Likewise the restorers of old British cars and the restylists of more recent models. They are taking something discarded by mainstream fashion and redeeming it – according to fashions defined by their own twilight aesthetics. For the restorer, it's often just another variety of antique collecting. But for the customiser it's a gesture of defiance, a loud V8 blast of impatience and irritation with the cosy order of bland, motorised Britain.

So – an individual horn sounds in the traffic jam of pre-packaged identity. But is it art?

Certainly, the self-styled restylists of California saw themselves as artists – some of them grew goatee beards to prove it. At the time, almost as many sullen introspective teenagers were drawn to the crucible of the car culture as arrived in the east clutching addresses in Greenwich Village.

Sensitive to the powerful imagery of the automobile, they wanted to action-paint their way on to the galleries of the freeway; to fashion from this sensitivity vivid sculptures of wheels and steel. They must have sensed, somehow, that Harley Earl's dream cars were a stronger, clearer, more dramatic statement of idealised form and line than, say, Saarinen's TWA terminal or even his new General Motors building – at any rate more of them had heard of Harley Earl than had heard of Saarinen.

The trouble is that cars rust, and airline terminals don't; therefore, while a car might be, in its time, very much like one of Barthes' great Gothic cathedrals, it soon becomes just a curio, such as the Daimler-Benz horseless carriage of 1896, a quaint, rare and expensive antique. The New York Museum of Modern Art preserves a post-war Pininfarina coupé or an Earl dream car because the form of these is part of what is currently deemed retro chic. But how many Regency charabancs could be described as art? Obviously, the car is not a work of art that lasts.

Nevertheless, car design fulfils most of Richard Hamilton's celebrated criteria for pop art: it is popular (designed for a mass audience), transient (a short-term solution), expendable (easily forgotten), witty, sexy, gimmicky, glamorous, mass-produced and manifestly big business. Hopefully, it will also ferry you from A to B. But since there is often so little practical difference between the way one car or another in the same class will do this, the buyer's choice is mainly determined by aesthetics – not even personal aesthetics so much as those shaped by the ad man's prescriptions of desire.

It follows from this that the customiser is ultimately saying more about the consumer society than about his sense of style, beauty and motional grace. Despite the supposed individuality of customising, for *every* work of personal flair there are two dozen stock customs, jacked-up, spliced and painted in much the same fashion.

As the largest product of the consumer society, the motor car has lent itself to more comments on that society than has, for instance, the soup can – although Andy Warhol soon got around to the motor car too. Choosing an obvious motif for his *Green Disaster*, he

A Detroit junk yard.

used a news photograph of a violent car crash in a series of endless, numbing repetitions. The car has even been the raw material of art: Rauschenberg's *Dylaby* was made from a tyre and a door; the French artist César uses a giant car crusher to create his sculptures – the various cubes of metal it produces. Other artists, such as Richard Hamilton, who used images from car advertising for *AAH!* and *Hers is a Lush Situation*, or Roy Lichtenstein with his blown-up comic-strip frame called *In the Car*, or Phil Garner, who built domestic furniture from old Chevrolets, have tended to parody the car and its associated imagery – either out of playful spite (as with Garner's furniture) or a dour and depressing malice.

Salvador Dali was being playful in the extreme when he mounted a large, voluptuous statue of a female warrior-goddess on the bonnet of a 1940s Cadillac, the curves of the displaced statue a surreal mimicry of the curves of the car. Dali's car is now the centrepiece of the Dali museum in Figueras. Dropping some pesetas into a coin slot illuminates the greenhouse interior of the car and sends a shower of water over the mass of foliage that has been allowed to grow inside, echoing the fate of its fellows at the Cadillac Ranch.

This fate echoes further in the choruses of popular songs. Chuck Berry's knowing sketches of teen car culture (*Maybellene, You Can't Catch Me, No Money Down*) and the Beach Boys' naive celebrations (*Little Deuce Coupe, Fun, Fun, Fun, Shut Down*) has given way to the epic eulogies of Bruce Springsteen (*Racing in the Streets, Thunder Road, Drive All Night* and *Wreck on the Highway*).

But perhaps the most devastating statement about the car culture is the one currently being made at a growing rate on the German *autobahns* – where otherwise well-adjusted men, seized by emotional crises, have discovered the bleak poetry of suicide by car.

Studies reveal that as many as one in twenty of the people who die on West Germany's roads may have *deliberately* chosen to do so. Sometimes there's a note to prove it, sometimes just the fact of a car in sound condition on a dry road that has suddenly veered off a bridge, or driven at high speed into a heavy lorry, or turned on to the wrong side of the road and crashed headlong into oncoming traffic.

The drivers are almost always men, according to research by Dr Alexander Balkanyi, who suggests it may be due to a man's intense relationship with his car. Commuting every day in the womb-like tranquilli-ty of the modern car provides a welcome escape from home and work, forms a bond of intimate solace. When he's at the wheel of his car may be the only time a man feels in control of his life. Dr Balkanyi compares these suicides to a lover's pact. 'A desperate man,' he surmises, 'wants not only to destroy himself but also the car which he loves above all other things.'

'If you fall in love with a machine,' wrote Lewis Mumford, 'there's something wrong with your love life.' And it seems that for some time now there was something amiss in the love life of the West. The motor car has been an ennervating and destructive influence in our lives, but the West has changed because of the car and now the car must change too.

Detroit will preserve its empire as best it can. Planned obsolescence was a good idea when the world was young, far more enjoyable than war or totalitarianism as a means of maintaining production. But finite resources have forced Detroit to cut its own throat by developing materials like Kevlar, five times stronger than steel and immune to fire and rust.

The car will endure, somehow, but the much more rapid and effortless means of social interaction promised by new micro-electronic media threaten to relegate its function to the purely recreational; where, as McLuhan prophesied, it should make a strong comeback. Surveying the long roads the car has travelled, you would be forgiven for thinking it was just a wonderful entertainment all along – but one that got diverted into pernicious social uses.

Manifestly a more fitting end than any other in our mass car culture, suicide by car, now that it has been exposed, will doubtless catch on. Those who have lived by the car shall die by the car – not always by accident nor even by design. The Federal Emergency Management Agency, who make post nuclear attack plans for the US, has even offered a scandalous and lonely piece of advice on digging a fallout shelter under a car.

Hopefully no American will suffer the cruel irony of having their cherished metal skins melt down on top of them. Nor with luck will anyone have to share the fate of the Australian movie hero *Mad Max*, doomed to roam perilous post-apocalypse roads scavenging for precious drops of gasoline in the last of the super-charged V8s.

In time, there will be fewer and fewer cars to roam in or shelter under; a bad dream in this generation but an inevitability in the lifetime of the next – and an end, if ever there could be, to the ingenious, fantastic, delightful parade of automania.

Manufactured in Italy